CAMBRIDGE CLASSICAL TEXTS AND COMMENTARIES

EDITORS

C. O. BRINK   R. D. DAWE   F. H. SANDBACH

ADVISORY BOARD

W. BÜHLER   K. J. DOVER   F. R. D. GOODYEAR
H. D. JOCELYN   E. J. KENNEY

21

THE EPIGRAMS OF RUFINUS

THE EPIGRAMS OF RUFINUS

EDITED WITH AN INTRODUCTION AND
COMMENTARY

BY

DENYS PAGE

CAMBRIDGE UNIVERSITY PRESS

CAMBRIDGE

LONDON · NEW YORK · MELBOURNE

Published by the Syndics of the Cambridge University Press
The Pitt Building, Trumpington Street, Cambridge CB2 1RP
Bentley House, 200 Euston Road, London NW1 2DB
32 East 57th Street, New York, NY 10022, USA
296 Beaconsfield Parade, Middle Park, Melbourne 3206, Australia

© Cambridge University Press 1978

First published 1978

Printed in Great Britain at the
University Press, Cambridge

Library of Congress Cataloguing in Publication Data
Rufinus.

The epigrams of Rufinus.

(Cambridge classical texts and commentaries; 21)
Includes indexes.
1. Epigrams, Greek. I. Page, Denys Lionel, Sir.
II. Title.
PA4407.R8A6 1978   888'.01   77-82512
ISBN 0 521 21767 9

A. S. F. GOW

κουφὰ δόσις ἀνδρὶ σοφῶι
ἀντὶ μόχθων παντοδαπῶν

CONTENTS

PREFACE

The justification for a monograph on Rufinus will not be immediately apparent to all; the work being done, I ask myself what it may have been.

Some preliminary study of him was necessary a decade ago in order to make sure that he should not be included in 'The Garland of Philip'; I made sure of that, and by the way found myself attracted to him, partly because nobody else has ever been, and partly because he seemed to me a talented but inscrutable writer, hard to place within any historical context.

The only continuous commentary on his poems by a scholar is that of C. F. W. Jacobs, published without much passion in 1801. Since then the world has not much troubled itself about him or even cared to make his acquaintance. Five perfunctory lines suffice for him in Schmid–Stählin; Lesky has no room for him; Kühner–Gerth's single reference to him is misplaced; the writer of a column on him in Pauly–Wissowa in 1931 must have had his mind on other topics.

And yet Rufinus is a lively and amusing author, above the average of the Anthology's contributors in the Christian era. There is much originality in his themes; his style is colourful and generally pleasing; a few hideous blunders increase interest in him. He is not much like anybody else in the Anthology; and his date is so uncertain that half a millennium is required to cover the range of guesses.

He was, in short, a total blank in my (or anyone else's) knowledge of the poets of the Anthology; and that, I suppose, is why I have spent a couple of years in his company.

I am much indebted to Professor F. H. Sandbach and Dr R. D. Dawe, who read a tiresome typescript and corrected the proofs; they suggested a number of improvements, all thankfully received.

Tarset, Northumberland   D.L.P.
October 1977

ABBREVIATIONS

A.P.	*Anthologia Palatina*
Beckby	H. Beckby, *Anthologia Graeca*, vol. i, 2nd ed. Munich 1966
Dübner	J. F. Dübner, *Anthologia Palatina*, vol. i, Paris 1864
HE	A. S. F. Gow and D. L. Page, *The Greek Anthology: Hellenistic Epigrams*, Cambridge 1965
Hecker 1843	A. Hecker, *Commentatio Critica de Anthologia Graeca*, Leyden 1843
Hecker 1852	A. Hecker, *Commentationis Criticae de Anthologia Graeca pars prior*, Leyden 1852
IEG	M. L. West, *Iambi et Elegi Graeci*, vol. i, Oxford 1971; vol. ii, 1972
Jacobs[1]	C. F. W. Jacobs, *Anthologia Graeca*, 13 vols., Leipzig 1794–1814; text of Rufinus in vol. iii 98–107, repeated from R. F. P. Brunck, *Analecta Veterum Poetarum Graecorum*, Strassburg 1772–6; commentary in vol. x 149–82
Jacobs[2]	*ibid.* vol. xiii 65–7 (*Addenda et Emendanda*)
Jacobs[3]	C. F. W. Jacobs, *Delectus Epigrammatum Graecorum*, Gotha and Erfurt 1826
Jacobs[4]	C. F. W. Jacobs, *Anthologia Graeca ad fidem cod. Pal. etc.*, Leipzig 1813–17
Mackail	J. W. Mackail, *Select Epigrams from the Greek Anthology*, 3rd ed. London 1911
Paton	W. R. Paton, *The Greek Anthology*, vol. i, London (Loeb) 1926
Peek	W. Peek, *Griechische Vers-Inschriften: 1. Grab-Epigramme*, Berlin 1955
PG	A. S. F. Gow and D. L. Page, *The Greek Anthology: The Garland of Philip*, Cambridge 1968
RE	Pauly–Wissowa, *Real-Encyclopädie* (1894–)

ABBREVIATIONS

| Stadtmüller | H. Stadtmüller, *Anthologia Graeca*, vol. i, Leipzig (Teubner) 1894 |
| Waltz | P. Waltz, *Anthologie Grecque*, vol. ii, Paris (Budé) 1938 |

INTRODUCTION

'SYLLOGE RUFINIANA'

Thirty-seven[1] amatory epigrams ascribed to Rufinus are preserved in the Fifth Book of the Palatine Anthology. No other information about this author has survived in any source. He does not appear in the Anthology's extracts from the *Garland* of Philip, which was published about A.D. 40; it is therefore a likely but not certain inference that the lower date-limit for Rufinus is the second half of the first century A.D. Guesses at the upper limit have ranged over half a millennium, from the second century[2] (more precisely, from the time of the Emperor Hadrian[3]) through the fourth[4] to the sixth.[5] There has been no full discussion of the subject; *obiter dicta* are the rule, to which the only notable exceptions are brief treatments of particular points by P. Sakolowski and M. Boas.[6]

It is convenient to consider first the environment in which the epigrams of Rufinus have been preserved. The problem is, in general, to determine the source from which Rufinus' epigrams entered the Palatine Anthology; and, in particular, to explain the context in which they are found there.

---

[1] This figure does not include *A.P.* 5.284, ascribed to 'Rufinus Domesticus' by the Palatine, to 'Rufus Domesticus' by Planudes, within an extract from the *Cycle* of Agathias. If the style of Rufinus did not (as it does) differentiate him from the *Cycle*-authors, his metrical technique (pp. 28ff.) would certainly do so.

[2] Th. Weigand, *Rh.Mus.* 3 (1845) 555; L. Schmidt and R. Reitzenstein, *RE* 1.2385.

[3] P. Sakolowski, *de Anth. Pal. quaest.* (diss. Lips. 1893) 68; Waltz, *Anthologie Grecque* (the Budé edition, Paris 1928–57) II 10; Beckby, *Anthologia Graeca* (Munich 1966) I 71.

[4] L. Sternbach, *Melet. Graeca* (Leipzig 1890) I 22; Weisshäupl, *Grabged. der gr. Anthol.* (Abh. Arch. Sem. d. Univ. Wien 7, 1889) 38.

[5] Jacobs, *Anthologia Graeca* XIII (Leipzig 1814) 947; Mackail, *Select Epigrams from the Greek Anthology* (London 1911) 334; Geffcken, *RE* Suppl. 5 (1931) 841–2.

[6] Sakolowski, *op. cit.*; Boas, *Philol.* 73 (1914) 1. Boas and Stadtmüller (Teubner ed. I.xxvii) are among the few who refrain from guessing at the upper limit for Rufinus.

The fact that Rufinus appears in the Anthology nowhere but in the opening section of the Fifth Book is not in itself surprising.[1] His epigrams are all amatory, and this Book is the proper place for them. *A.P.* 5.104–33 are a solid extract from Philip's *Garland*, 134–215 from Meleager's, 216–302 from the *Cycle* of Agathias. The end of the Book, 303–9, is a small miscellany. The only possible place for Rufinus is at the beginning or at the end (or, but less suitably, between two of the solid extracts). He is in fact put at the beginning. Nor is it surprising that he appears nowhere else in the Anthology. If he is not in Book XII, the only other context for amatory verse, we infer simply that few of his epigrams were paederastic (of the extant epigrams, only x and possibly vi would be suitable to Book XII).

If a more or less unbroken series of epigrams by Rufinus had appeared in Book V, there would be no great problem; we should have been content to infer that a collection of his epigrams was available to the compiler of the Palatine Anthology at some stage in the tradition. The problem arises from the fact that the epigrams of Rufinus are intermixed with epigrams by a variety of other authors in an apparently haphazard arrangement.

The only useful discussion of this matter is that of Marcus Boas in *Philologus* 73 (1914) 1–18. Boas took as his starting-point the fact that the first epigram in the medley which includes Rufinus, *A.P.* 5.2, is the only epigram in that medley which is 'headless', *i.e.* which has neither an author-name attached nor the explicit denial of one (ἀδέσποτον, ἄδηλον); and he suggested that the name which has dropped out is that of Rufinus. If that were so, the series in *A.P.* 5.2–103, preceding the solid extracts from the ancient anthologies, would both begin and end with Rufinus, just as the series which includes Strato in *A.P.* XII, a medley of many authors, begins and ends with Strato. Boas therefore recognised a 'Sylloge Rufiniana' of less shadowy definition than before, with its original beginning

---

[1] As it appears to Beckby, i 71: 'auffallend, aber noch ungeklärt, ist die Tatsache...'.

and end.[1] He supposed that a Rufinian anthology was available to Constantine Cephalas and supplemented by him with sundry epigrams from various sources. The text of the 'headless' epigram, *A.P.* 5.2, is as follows:

> τὴν καταφλεξίπολιν Σθενελαΐδα, τὴν βαρύμισθον,
> τὴν τοῖς βουλομένοις χρυσὸν ἐρευγομένην,
> γυμνήν μοι διὰ νυκτὸς ὅλης παρέκλινεν ὄνειρος,
> ἄχρι φίλης ἠοῦς προῖκα χαριζομένην.
> οὐκέτι γουνάσομαι τὴν βάρβαρον, οὐδ' ἐπ' ἐμαυτῶι
> κλαύσομαι, ὕπνον ἔχων κεῖνα χαριζόμενον.

The case for ascribing this epigram to Rufinus rests on four supports:[2]

(1) καταφλεξίπολιν is a compound of a very rare type, preposition + verbal element ending -σι + a further component. There are only two parallels in the Anthology, and it happens that one of them is in Rufinus, vii 2 διαλυσίφιλοι.

(2) ἄχρι φίλης ἠοῦς: φίλης seems inappropriate, and has been replaced by such unlikely conjectures as φίλημ' (Polak), φάους (F. G. Schmidt), φίλη σ' (Herwerden), βολῆς (Stadtmüller), and καλῆς (Hecker). Now it happens that the only close parallel in the Anthology is in Rufinus, viii 5, ἄχρι φίλης πολιῆς, where the same adjective seems equally inept.

(3) The apparently insensitive repetition[3] of χαριζόμενος at the end of two successive pentameters seems characteristic of Rufinus: xxxi 3–4 βάσις βάσιες, ἀστατέουσα ἄστατος; v 1, 3

---

[1] Boas thought it no accident that there are a couple of verbal resemblances between the first and the last epigrams in the series. 2.5 οὐκέτι γουνάσομαι, 103.1–2 ἄχρι τίνος σε γουνάσομαι; 2.6 κλαύσομαι, 103.1 παρακλαύσομαι.

[2] Boas with his usual candour admits that this is the whole of his case: p. 6, 'auf Grund dieser vier Indizien'.

[3] Boas is not justified in adding 1 3, 7 ὄμμα; the repeated words in iii ἄχρι, χεῖλος, ψαύω, στόμα; iv 4, 5 ἀποπλάσεται, πλασταί; v 3, 5 χρώς; vii 5, 6 προσέρχομαι, παρερχόμεθα; viii 2, 6 μήποτε; xviii 1, 2 Θάλεια, θαλερῆι; xviii 4, 5 κέκμηκα, ἀπόκαμε; xxi 2, 4 χρωτί; xxii 2, 5 γελᾶν, γελάσας; xxiii 1, 3 καλόν; xxviii 1, 5, 6 στέφος, στεψαμένη, στέφανος; xxviii 1, 6 ἄνθεσι, ἀνθεῖς; xxviii 5, 6 λῆξον, ληγεῖς; xxx 3, 6 γήραι, γηράσας. Some of these are deliberate and effective repetitions, the rest are unobtrusive and unobjectionable.

INTRODUCTION

and xxxiii 2, 4 σοβαρός; v 2, 6 and ix 4, 6 σπάταλος; xxv 4 καλὸν καλλοσύνης; xxxi 6 φλέξατε φλέγομαι.

(4) The epigram ends in a manner characteristic of Rufinus, οὐκέτι γουνάσομαι... : *cf.* xxv 3 οὐκέτι γυμνούμεσθα, x 5 μηκέτι μοι... προσέρχεο. These arguments fall far short of proof or even probability.

Indeed they are less persuasive than the general observation that the epigram rings rather more like Rufinus than any other author in the Anthology; and there is one other point which is worth notice.

Editors have found no acceptable explanation of, or substitute for, the word ἐρευγομένην in the second line. Neither defence[1] nor conjecture[2] deserves serious consideration. The word is unalterable, and has hitherto remained inexplicable.

The Lexicon distinguishes between 'ἐρεύγομαι (A), Latin *erugere, belch*', and 'ἐρεύγομαι (B), Latin *rugio, roar*'. Semantically these have a point in common inasmuch as both may be used of the human voice – 'belch' = 'pour forth', of effusive speech, and 'roar' = 'shout', of loud speech. In some contexts it is not clear which of the two verbs (if they really are distinct) is intended: Callimachus *fr.* 75.7 ἐξ ἂν ἐπεὶ καὶ τῶν ἤρυγες ἱστορίην, is ἐρεύγομαι (A); *cf. fr.* 714.4; Theocritus 13.58, (Heracles) τρὶς μὲν Ὕλαν ἄυσεν ὅσον βαθὺς ἤρυγε λαιμός, is ἐρεύγομαι (B), and so is Hom. *Il.* 20.403 *seqq.* ἤρυγεν ὡς ὅτε ταῦρος | ἤρυγεν... | ὡς ἄρα τόν γ' ἐρυγόντα λίπ' ὀστέα κτλ. In Matthew 13.35 ἐρεύξομαι κεκρυμμένα ἀπὸ καταβολῆς κόσμου, both 'pour forth' and 'cry aloud' are suitable; in Psalm 18(19).2, ἡμέρα τῆι ἡμέραι ἐρεύγεται ῥῆμα, 'pours forth' seems rather less suitable

---

[1] Meineke (*Del. Epigr.* 187) understood 'vomiting gold' to mean boasting of wealth; Jacobs[1] (xi 316–19) took it transitively, *quae viros cogebat aurum ipsi effundere*; Paton rendered 'whose breath smells of gold'.

[2] Jacobs[4] in his last edition still printed ἐρευγομένην but in the Preface ('Addenda' p. xxxii) conjectured ἀμεργομένην, and this is accepted by Waltz and Beckby; Hecker (1843, 27) conjectured ἐρυγγανέμεν or ἐρευγομένοις, rendering 'her who belonged to those who were willing to pour out gold' or 'her who belonged to those who desired her, who poured out gold'; later (1852, 111) he withdrew (as well he might) the latter alternative but re-affirmed his confidence in ἐρυγγανέμεν; Dübner conjectured ἐρεσσομένην (actually ἐρεττο-), Stadtmüller ἐρεπτομένην.

than 'cries aloud'. The entries in Hesychius, ἐρυγή·...φωνὴ καὶ βοή τις, and ἐρυγεῖν· φωνεῖν, suggest that the verb (whether 'A' or 'B') might mean little more than an emphatic 'utter', 'declare', as indeed it appears to mean in the Psalm just quoted. In *A.P.* 5.2.2 the only possible sense for τὴν τοῖς βουλομένοις χρυσὸν ἐρευγομένην is 'the one who, to those who desire her, shouts "gold!"';[1] and the use of the verb in this sense, which would pass without comment in the Septuagint or the New Testament, would be consistent with the ascription to Rufinus, whose Greek occasionally comes closer to the vernacular than that of other epigrammatists in the Anthology (see pp. 43f. below).

Against the ascription to Rufinus it may be said, firstly – a small matter – that 'Sthenelaïs' is not one of his numerous lady-names, and secondly – a very serious objection – that the case rests on uncertain speculation. It seems quite a likely guess; it is not, as Boas called it (p. 6), 'a certainty', and it ought not to be used as a base for the reconstruction of a 'Sylloge Rufiniana'.

Whether *A.P.* 5.2 is by Rufinus or not, the primary questions remain: did the compiler of the Palatine Anthology, whether Cephalas or a predecessor, inherit a collection of epigrams by Rufinus and himself mix them (or some of them) with epigrams from other sources? Or did he inherit an anthology in which this mixture was already made; and, if so, when was that anthology compiled?

The nature of the miscellany which includes Rufinus is revealed in the following catalogue:

t.α. = τοῦ αὐτοῦ   s.a.n. = sine auctoris nomine

---

[1] It looks as though Boissonade (*ap.* Dübner) was not far from the truth: *assidue et putide nummos usque loquentem;* but he was wrong about *assidue et putide.*

For χρυσὸν ἐρευγομένην = 'shouting "gold"', see Page, Eur. *Med.* 21 n.

cod. Palatinus	cod. Planudeus	Appendix Barberino-Vatic.
2 s.a.n.	τ.α. = Μελεάγρου	—
3 Ἀντιπάτρου Θεσσαλ.	τ.α. = Ἀντ. Θεσσ.	—
4 Φιλοδήμου	τ.α. = Φιλοδήμου	—
5 Στατυλλίου Φλάκκου	—	—
6 Καλλιμάχου	Καλλιμάχου	—
7 Ἀσκληπιάδου	τ.α. = Ἀσκληπ.	—
8 Μελεάγρου	τ.α. = Φιλοδήμου	—
9 Ῥουφίνου	1–2 τ.α. = Ῥουφ., 3–8 ἄδηλον	—
10 Ἀλκαίου	Ἀλκαίου	—
11 ἀδέσποτον	s.a.n.	—
12 Ῥουφίνου	τ.α. = Ῥουφίνου	—
13 Φιλοδήμου	τ.α. = Φιλοδήμου	—
14 Ῥουφίνου	τ.α. = Ῥουφίνου	—
15 τ.α. = Ῥουφίνου	τ.α. = Ῥουφίνου	—
16 Μάρκου Ἀργενταρίου	Μάρκου	—
17 Γαιτουλίκου	—	—
18 Ῥουφίνου	—	Ῥουφίνου
19 τ.α. = Ῥουφίνου	τ.α. = Ῥουφίνου	—
20 Ὀνέστου	Ὀνέστου	—
21 Ῥουφίνου	τ.α. = Ῥουφίνου	—
22 τ.α. = Ῥουφίνου	τ.α. = Ῥουφίνου	—
23 Καλλιμάχου	τ.α. = Ῥουφίνου	—
24 Φιλοδήμου	τ.α. = Φιλοδήμου	—
25 τ.α. = Φιλοδήμου	τ.α. = Φιλοδήμου	—
26 ἀδέσποτον	ἄδηλον	—
27 Ῥουφίνου	ἄδηλον	—
28 τ.α. = Ῥουφίνου	ἄδηλον	—
29 Κιλλάκτορος	—	—
30 Ἀντιπάτρου Θεσσαλ.	Ἀντιπάτρου Θεσσαλ.	—
31 τ.α. = Ἀντ. Θεσσ.	—	Κιλλάκτορος
32 Μάρκου Ἀργενταρίου	—	—
33 Παρμενίωνος	Παρμενίωνος	—
34 τ.α. = Παρμενίωνος	τ.α. = Παρμενίωνος	—
35 Ῥουφίνου	τ.α. = Ῥουφ. (tantum vv. 9–10)	Διονύσου
36 τ.α. = Ῥουφίνου	τ.α. = Ῥουφίνου	—
37 τ.α. = Ῥουφίνου	—	Ῥουφίνου
38 Νικάρχου	—	—
39 τ.α. = Νικάρχου	Νικάρχου	—

cod. Palatinus	cod. Planudeus	Appendix Barberino-Vatic.
40 τ.α. = Νικάρχου	τ.α. = Νικάρχου	—
41 'Ρουφίνου	τ.α. = 'Ρουφίνου	τ.α. = 'Ρουφίνου
42 τ.α. = 'Ρουφίνου	s.a.n.	—
43 τ.α. = 'Ρουφίνου	τ.α. = 'Ρουφίνου	—
44 τ.α. = 'Ρουφίνου	—	—
45 Κιλλάκτορος	—	—
46 Φιλοδήμου	—	—
47 'Ρουφίνου	—	—
48 τ.α. = 'Ρουφίνου	s.a.n.	—
49 τοῦ δικαίου Γάλλου	—	—
50 ἀδέσποτον	—	'Ρουφίνου
51 ἀδέσποτον	s.a.n.	—
52 Διοσκορίδου	—	—
53 τ.α. = Διοσκορ.	—	—
54 τ.α. = Διοσκορ.	—	—
55 τ.α. = Διοσκορ.	—	—
56 τ.α. = Διοσκορ.	s.a.n.	—
57 Μελεάγρου	—	—
58 'Αρχίου	—	—
59 τ.α. = 'Αρχίου	s.a.n.	—
60 'Ρουφίνου	—	τ.α. = 'Ρουφίνου
61 τ.α. = 'Ρουφίνου	—	—
62 τ.α. = 'Ρουφίνου	—	—
63 Μάρκου 'Αργενταρίου	—	—
64 'Ασκληπιάδου	τ.α. = 'Ασκληπ.	
65 ἀδέσποτον	ἄδηλον	—
66 ἀδέσποτον P, 'Ρουφίνου C	τ.α. = 'Ρουφίνου	—
67 Καπίτωνος	τ.α. = Νικάρχου	
68 Λουκιλλίου, οἱ δὲ Πολέμωνος	Λουκιλλίου	—
69 'Ρουφίνου	'Ρουφίνου	—
70 τ.α. = 'Ρουφίνου	τ.α. = 'Ρουφίνου	—
71 τ.α. = 'Ρουφ. P, Παλλαδᾶ J, τ.α. = οἱ δὲ Παλλαδᾶ C	—	Παλλαδᾶ
72 τ.α. = Παλλαδᾶ	—	—
73 'Ρουφίνου	—	—
74 τ.α. = 'Ρουφίνου	τ.α. = 'Ρουφίνου	—
75 τ.α. = 'Ρουφίνου	τ.α. = 'Ρουφίνου	—

cod. Palatinus	cod. Planudeus	Appendix Barberino-Vatic.
76 τ.α. = Ῥουφίνου	τ.α. = Ῥουφίνου	—
77 τ.α. = Ῥουφίνου	—	ἄδηλον
78 Πλάτωνος	—	—
79 τ.α. = Πλάτωνος	s.a.n.	—
80 τ.α. = Πλάτωνος	τ.α. = Φιλοδήμου	—
81 Διονυσίου Σοφιστοῦ	Διονυσίου Σοφιστοῦ	—
82 ἀδέσποτον	τ.α. = Μελεάγρου	Διονύσου
83 ἀδέσποτον	τ.α. = Διονυσίου Σοφ.	—
84 ἀδέσποτον	(cum 83 coniunctum)	—
85 Ἀσκληπιάδου	s.a.n.	—
86 Κλαυδιανοῦ	—	—
87 Ῥουφίνου	τ.α. = Ῥουφίνου	—
88 τ.α. = Ῥουφίνου	τ.α. = Ῥουφίνου	—
89 Μάρκου Ἀργενταρίου	τ.α. = Ῥουφίνου	—
90 ἀδέσποτον	τ.α. = Ῥουφίνου	—
91 ἀδέσποτον	s.a.n.	—
92 Ῥουφίνου	τ.α. = Ῥουφίνου	—
93 τ.α. = Ῥουφίνου	τ.α. = Ῥουφίνου	—
94 τ.α. = Ῥουφίνου	τ.α. = Ῥουφίνου	—
95 ἀδέσποτον	τ.α. = Ῥουφίνου	—
96 Μελεάγρου	—	Μελεάγρου
97 Ῥουφίνου	τ.α. = Ῥουφίνου	—
98 ἄδηλον, οἱ δὲ Ἀρχίου	(cum 67 coniunctum)	—
99 ἄδηλον	—	Μελεάγρου
100 ἄδηλον	ἄδηλον	—
101 ἀδέσποτον	ἄδηλον	—
102 Μάρκου Ἀργενταρίου	τ.α. = Μάρκου Ἀργεντ.	—
103 Ῥουφίνου	τ.α. = Ῥουφίνου	—

The most obvious points to be noticed are

(a) that this section includes authors of very different types and from very different times – only not from the *Cycle* of Agathias. In addition to Rufinus, there appear authors from the *Garlands* of Meleager and Philip; Gaetulicus, probably of the first half of the first century A.D.; Lucillius and Nicarchus, satirical epigrammatists of the middle and later parts of the first century A.D.; Palladas, of the fourth century; and a number of authors elsewhere seldom or never represented in the Anthology (Capito, Cillactor, Claudianus, Dionysius Sophistes, Gallus);

(b) that the arrangement is unsystematic.[1]

In a number of places two epigrams similar in theme are juxtaposed: 27–8, the revenge of the passing years; 35–6, beauty-competitions; 54–5, sexual intercourse; 79–80, the apple-motif (78–80 came into the Anthology direct, and in the same order, from Diogenes Laertius; 83–4 direct from the scholia on Dio Chrysostom); 90–1, the unguent; 94–5, girls beautiful as goddesses or Graces; 97–8, the bow and arrows of Eros. The connection is thinner between 12 and 13, on the theme of old age but in very different contexts; and between 16 and 17, the separation of lovers, again in very different contexts.[2]

There are very few places where more than two epigrams similar in theme are juxtaposed: 3–8, closely related extracts

---

[1] In considering this matter I have noted the observations of Sakolowski, approved by Stadtmüller (i.xxvi n.), concerning 'alphabetical' order in the extracts from Philip. The facts plainly refute the notion that traces of the original order are discernible. Of the 16 epigrams (including Statyllius) ascribed in P to Philippan authors, one sequence of 3 (3–5) and one of 5 (30–4) are arranged by theme, with consequent disruption of the order of Philip's *Garland*. The initials of the Philippan epigrams scattered through 2–103 run ο τ α ε μ ο ο π χ π ε ο χ α ο τ. The notion that the sequences within this, ε μ ο ο π χ and α ο τ, result from taking epigrams from the *Garland* in the alphabetical order of that source, is an illusion. The π χ in ε μ ο ο π χ owe their position to their theme and cohere with what follows, not with what precedes. The sequence ε μ ο ο π χ is as clearly fortuitous as 87–93 α ε ο π π υ ω, which is shown to be mere chance by the fact that the epigrams come from miscellaneous sources.

[2] Boas' discussion of this matter is unsatisfactory. He admits that the arrangement is incoherent from 5.44 onwards but finds more order than really exists in 2–43 (*e.g.* 23 and 24 are related because Κωνώπιον in 23 suggests κώνωψ, and ἀναιδής in 24 is an epithet suitable to the κώνωψ; why 9 and 10 are placed together is said to be self-evident, though they seem wholly unrelated; 15 and 16 are said to be connected by the idea of 'search' – in 15, for a sculptor to portray the beloved, in 16 for the beloved herself); and he is arbitrary in dealing with recalcitrant epigrams (*e.g.* 44, because it is unrelated to 43, must be a later intrusion). The picture is further confused by unconvincing and sometimes quite arbitrary addition (11, 26, 54–6, 98) or subtraction (37, 42, 44) of the name of Rufinus in the headings.

11

from the *Garlands* of Meleager and Philip (the lamp-motif is common to 4, 5, 7, and 8, the oath-motif to 5, 6, 7, and 8). 23–5: 23, the cruel beauty; 24, the woman from whom one had better run; 25, the woman whom it is dangerous to approach. 29–34: all have the mercenary-love motif. To these may be added 18–20, which have the preference-motif in common (18, slave or lady; 19, boys or girls; 20, young, ripe, or old); and perhaps, though they are more loosely connected, 57–9, on various aspects of Eros.

More striking are the numerous missed opportunities; epigrams on the same theme are more or less widely separated: 9 and 17, on the rare theme of lovers separated by the sea; both have the 'return-tomorrow' motif; 9 and 40, the latter being the nearest parallel in the Anthology to the epistle-form of 9; 12, 74, 85, 103, 'enjoy love while you are young'; 13, 26, 48, 62, a woman ageing but still beautiful; 14, 78, the kiss that affects the soul; 18–20 and 37–8, the preference-motif; 21, 23, 27, 28, 76, 92, the revenge of the passing years; 22, 100, the λάτρις Ἔρωτος; 41, 43, the expelled adulteress; 46, 101, street-scenes; 49, 54–5, sexual intercourse; 5–8, 52, the oath; 60, 73, the bathing beauty; 29–34, 63, mercenary love; 68, 88, 97, mutual love; 70, 94–5, the girl, the goddesses, and the Graces.

The epigrams of Rufinus himself are scattered more or less at random. They occur singly in five places, two together in seven, three together in three, and four together in two places. Epigrams on the same or similar themes are not as a rule put together. Two epigrams on beauty-competitions are indeed juxtaposed (35–6), but age's revenge on the proud beauty is the subject of widely separated epigrams (21, 27, 76, 92, 103); 41 and 43, on the same theme, are separated by an irrelevant epigram; 48 and 62, on a woman ageing but still beautiful, are widely separated, and so are 60 and 73, on the bathing beauty, and 88 and 97, on mutual love.

Speculation about the source of *A.P.* 5.2–103 must take account of four points:

(1) The smallness of the number of Rufinus-epigrams, 37 in a section containing 102, suggests rather an anthology-com-

ponent than a separate Rufinus-collection as the source, and so does the fact that the Rufinus-epigrams are scattered throughout the section, not included *en bloc*.[1]

(2) The *Cycle* of Agathias is not represented in this section. If the non-Rufinian epigrams were added by Cephalas or by any predecessor since the seventh century, why did he exclude the *Cycle* while admitting epigrams from so many other sources – the *Garland* of Meleager, the *Garland* of Philip, the anthology of satirical epigrams, Diogenes Laertius (for 78–80), the scholia on Chrysostom (for 83–4), and Palladas? The likely reason why the *Cycle* is not present is because the non-Rufinian epigrams were selected before the *Cycle* existed; that is to say, the source of this section was an anthology, of which Rufinus was a principal component, made before the middle of the sixth century A.D.

(3) None of the epigrams from the Garlands of Meleager and Philip in this section recurs in the main sequences from those *Garlands* in *A.P.* 5.134–215 and 104–33. This cannot be fortuitous; what is the likeliest explanation?

If Cephalas possessed an anthology comprising Rufinus together with other amatory poets, especially those of the *Garlands*, there is no problem. He would merely need to subtract those *Garland*-epigrams which he was including in the main sequences; and it may be added that such subtraction would be likely to disrupt such principles of arrangement as may have existed in the source, causing the mixture of coherence and incoherence described above.

If on the other hand Cephalas himself added the non-Rufinian epigrams in *A.P.* 5.2–103, his procedure will seem much less rational. He must re-peruse the *Garlands* and select amatory epigrams excluded from the main sequences (for I suppose that the main sequences are the heart and soul of the Book, and 2–103 an appendage); but there is no apparent reason why the *Garland* epigrams deemed worthy of inclusion in 2–103 should have been omitted from the main sequences, or why they

---

[1] Boas suggests that Cephalas wished to avoid blocks of epigrams by one author; but he frequently includes such blocks elsewhere.

should have been selected to occupy their present positions in 2–103.

(4) The main source for Planudes' selection of epigrams corresponding to *A.P.* V was not the Palatine manuscript but some other source which differed from the Palatine especially in its headings to epigrams. If 2–103 were first assembled in their present form by Cephalas, it is not likely that so discrepant a copy of his work would have emerged in the interval between him and Planudes.

RUFINUS IN THE PLANUDEAN MANUSCRIPT

Amatory epigrams are assembled in the Seventh Chapter of the Planudean Anthology. The relation of this Chapter to the Palatine's Fifth Book is in most respects close, but in one respect Planudes differs from the Palatine to such an extent that a source for Planudes independent of the Palatine must be inferred.

Planudes' Seventh Chapter consists for the most part of epigrams arranged in orderly blocks interrupted from time to time by small disorderly sequences. The Chapter begins with a series of 27 epigrams by authors of Meleager's *Garland*, 19 of them ascribed to Meleager, 2 to Asclepiades, 1 to 'Asclepiades or Posidippus', 1 each to Posidippus, Leonidas, and Simonides, and 2 ἄδηλα. It continues with a series from the *Cycle* of Agathias, 58 epigrams, followed by 16 ascribed to Philodemus. A single epigram by Antiphilus, a Philippan author, intervenes, then come 13 by Meleager, 3 by Asclepiades and 2 by Posidippus. Then follows a small medley, 1 each from 'Rufus', Antiphilus and Lucillius. These are followed by a solid block of 28 epigrams ascribed to Rufinus. Thereafter, 2 ascribed to Dionysius Sophistes are followed by a block of authors from Philip's *Garland* – Maccius 3, Argentarius 4, Antipater of Thessalonica 2, and Parmenion 2. Then comes another small medley, 1 each from Callimachus, Alcaeus and Honestus, 3 from Nicarchus, 1 each from Argentarius, Crinagoras and

Bassus. Then comes a block of epigrams headed ἄδηλον, then a curious intruder, *A.Plan.* 388. The Chapter ends with 13 epigrams which recur in *A.P.* XII followed by 12 which recur in *A.P.* V, all without any heading at all.

Some of the differences between the Palatine and the Planudean in the arrangement of epigrams appear to be related to differences in the headings. Although such differences in the Anthology at large are often obviously the result of oversight or error by Planudes, it must be remembered that Planudes used sources independent of the Palatine, and that he is occasionally the sole authority for author-names which are probably correct and are unlikely to be conjectural.[1]

In *A.P.* V the differences between P and Pl may be discussed under the following headings:

(1) P offers alternatives and Pl gives only one of them: 68 Λουκιλλίου, οἱ δὲ Πολέμωνος τοῦ Ποντικοῦ P, Λουκιλλίου Pl; 209 Ποσιδίππου ἢ ᾿Ασκληπιάδου P, Ποσειδίππου Pl; 208 τοῦ αὐτοῦ (= ᾿Ασκληπιάδου) ἢ μᾶλλον Φιλοδήμου P, τοῦ αὐτοῦ (= Φιλοδήμου) Pl.

(2) Pl continues a heading τοῦ αὐτοῦ beyond the point at which it should have changed: 23 Καλλιμάχου P, τοῦ αὐτοῦ (= ῾Ρουφίνου) Pl; two epigrams by Rufinus precede 23 in P, both are copied by Pl but the change of author at 23 is overlooked. 83 and 84, separate epigrams in P, are both headed ἀδέσποτον; Pl combines them as a single epigram with the heading τοῦ αὐτοῦ (= Διονυσίου Σοφιστοῦ); 81 is ascribed to Dionysius Sophistes in both P and Pl, and that heading is presumably the source of the heading of 83 in Pl.[2] 89 Μάρκου ᾿Αργενταρίου P, τοῦ αὐτοῦ (= ῾Ρουφίνου) Pl; two epigrams by Rufinus precede 89 in P, both are copied by Pl but the change of author at 89 is overlooked. The same carelessness explains the ascription of the next epigram, 90, to Rufinus in Pl (τοῦ αὐτοῦ; ἀδέσποτον P). 95 ἀδέσποτον P, τοῦ αὐτοῦ (= ῾Ρουφίνου) Pl; three epigrams by Rufinus precede in P, all are copied

---

[1] See Gow & Page, *The Garland of Philip* (Cambridge 1968) i.li–liii.
[2] The intervening epigram, 82, ἀδέσποτον in P, is headed τοῦ αὐτοῦ in Pl, where in fact it follows an epigram by Meleager.

by Pl but the change of author at 95 is overlooked. 113 Μάρκου Ἀργενταρίου P, τοῦ αὐτοῦ (= Φιλοδήμου) Pl; an epigram by Philodemus precedes 113 in P, it is copied by Pl but the change of authors at 113 and 114 is overlooked.

The above headings in Pl should be regarded as having no authority, being the result of mere carelessness. The explanation of the following differences is much less obvious:

(3) 67 Καπίτωνος P, τοῦ αὐτοῦ (= Νικάρχου) Pl: P has three epigrams by Nicarchus, 38–40, widely separated from the Capito-epigram; Pl copied the Nicarchus-epigrams 39 and 40, and there is no obvious reason why he should jump a long way forward to the Capito-epigram, or why, if he did so, he should ascribe it to Nicarchus. 80 τοῦ αὐτοῦ (= Πλάτωνος) P, τοῦ αὐτοῦ (= Φιλοδήμου) Pl: there is no epigram by Philodemus in the vicinity in P, and there is no obvious reason why Pl should have inserted this epigram between the two by Philodemus, 306 and 4. 241 Παύλου Σιλεντιαρίου P, τοῦ αὐτοῦ (= Ἀγαθίου) Pl: there is no obvious reason why Planudes should have inserted this epigram into a series by Agathias (it is the only discrepancy between P and Pl in the *Cycle*-epigrams of Book V, except the difference between 'Rufinus' and 'Rufus' at 284).

(4) In three places an epigram headless in P has an author-name in Pl:

2 s.a.n. P, τοῦ αὐτοῦ (= Μελεάγρου) Pl: the ascription to Meleager is certainly false, and this may be an error of the class of (2) above; the epigram is preceded in Pl by one ascribed in Pl to Meleager but in P to Strato.

141 s.a.n. P, τοῦ αὐτοῦ (= Μελεάγρου) Pl, and 143 s.a.n. P, Μελεάγρου Pl: epigrams by Meleager precede and follow in P, and both 141 and 143 name Meleager's beloved Heliodora, so the ascriptions in Pl are the most obvious of emendations.

So far, although we cannot explain the discrepancies in 2, 67, 80, and 241, confusion, carelessness or conjecture on the part of Planudes remain possible causes. In the following category we must continue to distinguish between the explicable and the obscure:

(5) There are three places where P and Pl offer different author-names (as distinguished from differences involving the use of τοῦ αὐτοῦ).

161 Ἡδύλου ἢ ᾽Ασκληπιάδου P, Σιμωνίδου Pl: 161 is very like 159, ascribed to Simonides in both P and Pl, so that heading may be the source of the error in Pl.

189 ᾽Ασκληπιάδου P, Μελεάγρου Pl: the following epigram in P is by Meleager, and mere carelessness by Pl is an obvious possibility.

215 τοῦ αὐτοῦ Μελεάγρου P, Ποσειδίππου Pl: the context in P is 211 Posidippus, 212 Meleager, 213 Posidippus, 214 Meleager, and mere carelessness on the part of Planudes is again a possibility.

There remain two places, involving five epigrams, where the difference seems inexplicable unless Pl was following a source independent of P:

   27 Ῥουφίνου P, ἄδηλον Pl
   28 τοῦ αὐτοῦ (= Ῥουφίνου) P, ἄδηλον Pl
   105 τοῦ αὐτοῦ (= Μάρκου ᾽Αργενταρίου) P, ἄδηλον Pl
   106 Διοτίμου Μιλησίου P, ἄδηλον Pl
   107 Φιλοδήμου P, ἄδηλον Pl

It is quite beyond our comprehension why Planudes, if he was copying from P, should explicitly mark as being of uncertain authorship five epigrams plainly – and, we suppose, correctly – attributed to their authors in P.

The foregoing raises a question about the block of ἄδηλα and the block of headless epigrams in Chapter VII of Planudes.

Not quite all Planudes' ἄδηλα are included in the former block (Ch. VII 174–84): there are two ἄδηλα in the opening series (VII 3 = *A.P.* 5.142 and VII 14 = *A.P.* 5.168): but plainly Planudes intended to group all his ἄδηλα together and his headless epigrams together at the end of his Chapter. In the case of the headless epigrams he has been wholly consistent: that is to say, the omission of headings in Pl is not the result of carelessness – indeed the arrangement of these epigrams is the outcome of careful planning; Planudes deliberately assembled all epigrams which lacked a heading in his source, in order

17

to group them together at the end of his Chapter; he also assembled epigrams marked ἀδέσποτον or ἄδηλον in his source
(though not quite all of them) and these he put together just
before the headless epigrams. Plainly the source for these epigrams was not the Palatine: for six of the group of ten ἄδηλα[1]
in Pl have author-names in P,[2] and of the twenty-five epigrams headless in Pl, fifteen have author-names in P and none
is headless.[3]

This is a surprising conclusion. The arrangement of the great
majority of the epigrams in Chapter vii of Planudes reflects a
source in which the order was the same as that of the Palatine,
and the occasional disruptions of that order are for the most
part easily explicable. Apart from the blocks of ἄδηλα and
headless epigrams, there are very few divergent ascriptions in
Pl which seem plausible evidence for the use of a source
independent of P. But the evidence of these two blocks is, as set
out above, decisive. An anthologist who made it his business to
collect all ἄδηλα and all headless epigrams in order to group
them together at the end of his selection, could not possibly have
compiled the lists of ἄδηλα and of headless epigrams as presented
to us by Planudes if his principal source for headings was the
Palatine manuscript.

The general conclusions are:

(a) That *A.P.* 5.2–103 represent an anthology of amatory
epigrams, including Rufinus, compiled before the time of
Agathias; there is no evidence to show whether the anthology
was compiled by Rufinus himself.

(b) That the anthology was preserved into the later Byzantine
world in at least two copies, which differed appreciably in
their epigram-headings.[4]

---

[1] Not counting Pl ch. vii 174 = *A.P.* 5.9.3–8, the continuation of vii 137 =
5.9.1–2.

[2] Of the other four, three are ἀδέσποτα, one ἄδηλον in P.

[3] Three are ἀδέσποτα, seven ἄδηλα, in P.

[4] I draw attention to certain contrasts between the first two thirds and the last
third of the section 5.2–103; one can only speculate about their significance:
(a) 2–64 include 26 epigrams ascribed in P to authors from the two
Garlands (29 if Statyllius and Archias are included); 65–103 include only

INTRODUCTION

RUFINUS AND AUSONIUS

Some of Ausonius' epigrams are versions of the Greek in the Anthology. The version may be a close translation, as in Ausonius xiv = *A.P.* 9.44, xii = *Plan.* 318, xlii = *Plan.* 263, lxxxi = *A.P.* 11.113; or it may take a few liberties, as in xxxv = *A.P.* 9.18, lxiv = *Plan.* 174, lxv = *A.P.* 6.1, lix = 11.225, xcvi = 5.158; or it may be partly translation, partly original, as in lxvii, where the first couplet translates *Plan.* 162 but the next two couplets are independent, and xliii, where the first and last couplets of *A.P.* 7.229 are translated but the middles are very different, and xxxiii, which is a loose rendering of *Plan.* 275.

Identification of particular Anthology-models in Ausonius may be illusory. The series of epigrams (lxviii–lxxv) on Myron's bronze heifer are all suggested by, and may be translations of, Greek models; but hardly any of them[1] are translations of the epigrams extant in the Anthology's series (9.713–42). Palladas' joke about the masculine, feminine, and neuter children of the schoolmaster's daughter (9.489) reappears in a Roman setting in Ausonius lxi; Ausonius and Palladas were contemporary, and Ausonius may have known this epigram by Palladas, but the truth may be that each is making his own version of a popular joke. The notion of Sappho as a tenth Muse was doubtless a commonplace, and it is not likely that Ausonius li is directly inspired by *A.P.* 9.506 or 9.571.7–8. A warning against hasty recognition of particular Greek models for Ausonius is given by xvi, which some have called a version of *A.P.* 10.30, ὠκεῖαι Χάριτες κτλ., although the heading in Ausonius shows that the model was an otherwise unknown epigram beginning ἁ χάρις ἁ βραδύπους ἄχαρις χάρις.

7 from these sources, and 3 of these are in the Plato-series derived from Diogenes Laertius.

(*b*) 2–64 include only 3 epigrams headed ἀδέσποτον, none ἄδηλον; 65–103 include a large proportion of anonymous epigrams – 8 ἀδέσποτα and 2 ἄδηλα, in addition to 66, originally ἀδέσποτον in P, and 98, ἄδηλον, οἱ δὲ 'Αρχίου.

(*c*) The only substantial blocks of epigrams connected by similarity of theme, 2–8 and 29–34, occur early in the section.

[1] Ep. 63 translates *A.P.* 9.730.

This warning is relevant when the relation of Ausonius xc to *A.P.* 5.68 is considered:

Ausonius xc

> hoc quod amare vocant solve aut misceto, Cupido:
> aut neutrum flammis ure vel ure duos.

A.P. 5.68 (Λουκιλλίου, οἱ δὲ Πολέμωνος)

> ἢ τὸ φιλεῖν περίγραψον, Ἔρως, ὅλον, ἢ τὸ φιλεῖσθαι
> πρόσθες, ἵν' ἢ λύσῃς τὸν πόθον ἢ κεράσῃς.

These may be rather two variations on a common theme than translation of this particular Greek epigram by the Latin. The theme, which may have been commonplace, ἢ λῦσον ἢ κέρασον τὸν ἔρωτα, appears in both, but the distinguishing feature of the Greek – the novel metaphor in ἢ περίγραψον ἢ πρόσθες – is not represented at all in Ausonius.

The relation between Ausonius xci and Rufinus XXXII is now to be considered against this background:

Ausonius xci

> aut restingue ignem quo torreor, alma Dione,
> aut transire iube, vel fac utrimque parem.

Rufinus 5.88 = XXXII

> εἰ δυσὶν οὐκ ἴσχυσας ἴσην φλόγα, πυρφόρε, καῦσαι,
> τὴν ἐνὶ καιομένην ἢ σβέσον ἢ μετάθες.

Ausonius' version is plainly translation of Rufinus, not variation on a common theme. All but one of the features of the Greek recur in the Latin: *utrimque parem* (*ignem*) represents δυσὶν ἴσην φλόγα; *aut restingue aut transire iube* translates ἢ σβέσον ἢ μετάθες; τὴν ἐνὶ καιομένην, equivalent to ἧι ἐγὼ μόνος καίομαι, is rendered by *quo torreor*. The only discrepancy is *alma Dione* for πυρφόρε. Ausonius may well have thought *ignem...ignifer* inelegant, and simply replaced the latter word by something different (the point of the epigram is not affected). It seems at first sight strange that he did not solve his little problem by writing *quo torreor ipse, Cupido*; and especially strange that he should choose *Dione*. But Ausonius has a mind of his own, and quite often admits a minor variation into an otherwise close translation.

It is highly probable that Ausonius, the translator of numerous Anthology-epigrams, is the later of the two. Neither his birth-year nor his death-year is known, but it is certain that he was active from *c.* 333 to *c.* 393, and the limits 310 for his birth and 395 for his death cannot be more than a few years wrong. We conclude that an epigram by Rufinus was in circulation before the death of Ausonius, *i.e.* before the last decade of the fourth century. How long before, we do not yet know. The second and third centuries are not intrinsically likelier than the fourth: Ausonius translated at least one epigram by his contemporary Palladas (xii = *Plan.* 317).

As the verdict is already given, the evidence of Ausonius xxxiv is not of much importance; and it is fortunate that this is so, because the relation of that epigram to Rufinus vii is hard to judge. The theme is the same in both (*fugaces anni*), and the beginnings are alike – οὐκ ἔλεγον, Προδίκη, γηράσκομεν; in Rufinus, *dicebam tibi, Galla, senescimus* in Ausonius. This looks very like translation, but there is no resemblance between the two in the remainder, and mere coincidence cannot be quite ruled out; there is no other example in Ausonius of an epigram beginning with a close translation of a short phrase and continuing independently at some length.

RUFINUS AND CLAUDIAN

The evidence of Ausonius would be reinforced by that of Claudian if the ascription of *A.P.* 5.50 were free from doubt:
Claudian, *carm. min.* xv (lxxxix)

> paupertas me saeva domat dirusque Cupido:
> sed toleranda fames, non tolerandus amor.

A.P. 5.50 = Rufinus xx

> καὶ πενίη καὶ ἔρως δύο μοι κακά· καὶ τὸ μὲν οἴσω
> κούφως, πῦρ δὲ φέρειν Κύπριδος οὐ δύναμαι.

This is plainly translation, not independent writing on a common theme. Claudian was born *c.* 370 and died probably in the decade following 410. His testimony would therefore repeat what we have learnt from Ausonius.

As it happens, *A.P.* 5.50 is marked ἀδέσποτον in the Palatine, and the ascription to Rufinus appears only in the *Appendix Barberino-Vaticana*; how much confidence should we have in this source?

ASCRIPTIONS IN THE APPENDIX BARBERINO-VATICANA

The Palatine and the Appendix have 52 epigrams[1] in common. In two (App. 8 = 12.237 and 53 = 5.187) the Appendix has omitted the first line and the heading. Of the remaining 50, 35[2] agree about the authorship and 15 disagree. The Appendix comes badly out of a comparison of disagreements:

A.P. 12.65 Μελεάγρου = App. 3 ἄδηλον: plainly by Meleager, as the name Myiscus proves; P has preserved the correct heading.

5.172 τοῦ αὐτοῦ *sc.* Μελεάγρου = App. 9 ἄδηλον: undoubtedly by Meleager; the Appendix is again the inferior.

5.31 τοῦ αὐτοῦ *sc.* Ἀντιπάτρου Θεσσαλονικέως = App. 10 Κιλλάκτορος: 5.29 is ascribed to Cillactor in P, and that heading may be the source of error in the Appendix.

5.82 ἀδέσποτον = App. 12 Διονυσίου: the preceding epigram in P is ascribed to Dionysius; that heading may have been carelessly repeated in the Appendix or its source.

5.99 ἄδηλον = App. 18 Μελεάγρου: certainly not by Meleager; the Appendix is wrong.

5.244 Παύλου Σιλεντιαρίου = App. 21 Ἐρατοσθένους: the names *Doris* and *Galatea* recur in Paulus but not in Eratosthenes; P is almost certainly correct.

5.77 Ῥουφίνου = App. 23 ἄδηλον: certainly not by Rufinus; the Appendix has the advantage.

12.79 ἄδηλον = App. 35 Μελεάγρου: almost certainly not by Meleager (whose lover-names do not include 'Antipatros'); the Appendix is wrong.

[1] Not counting App. 7 (not an epigram, and not in P or Pl) or 45 (ascribed to Numenius; a close imitation of Meleager 12.60, but it is not the same epigram).

[2] In these I include (*a*) App. 4, 5, 6 = 12.1, 2, 4: App. heads the first of these 'Strato' but does not repeat this for the next two; P has only the general Book-heading 'Strato of Sardis' for the first, heads the second 'Strato' and the third 'the same'. (*b*) App. 54 = 5.71: App. agrees with J ('Palladas') against P ('Rufinus').

5.243 Μακεδονίου ὑπάτου = App. 36 Ἐρατοσθένους: no means of deciding.
5.246 Παύλου Σιλεντιαρίου = App. 38 Ἐρατοσθένους: Sternbach (*App.B.-V.* 63) shows that the phrasing is very like that of Paulus; P is preferable.
5.305 ἄδηλον = App. 43 Ἀγαθίου: surely not by Agathias; the Appendix probably wrong.
12.17 ἄδηλον = App. 44 Ἀσκληπιάδου ἢ Ποσιδίππου: no means of deciding.
(5.50 = App. 49: this is the epigram translated by Claudian.)
5.158 Ἀσκληπιάδου = App. 51 ἄδηλον: the ascription to Asclepiades is plausible.
5.186 Ποσειδίππου = App. 52 ἄδηλον: the ascription to Posidippus is plausible.

It appears that, where the two disagree, P is most often plainly correct or at least preferable. It is thus the more likely of the two to have preserved the proper heading in *A.P.* 5.50; but the Appendix was right on one occasion (5.77 = 23), and may be right here too.

RUFINUS AND STRATO

The lower limit for the date of Rufinus is much harder to define than the upper. Evidence has been sought in his relation to the epigrammatist Strato of Sardis, and this will now be considered. The closest apparent points of contact are:

(*a*) Rufinus 1

> Ῥουφῖνος τῆι 'μῆι γλυκερωτάτηι Ἐλπίδι πολλά
> χαίρειν, εἰ χαίρειν χωρὶς ἐμοῦ δύνασαι.
> οὐκέτι βαστάζω, μὰ τὰ σ' ὄμματα, τὴν φιλέρημον
> καὶ τὴν μουνολεχῆ σεῖο διαζυγίην,
> 5   ἀλλ' αἰεὶ δακρύοισι πεφυρμένος ἢ 'πὶ Κορησσόν
> ἔρχομαι ἢ μεγάλης νηὸν ἐς Ἀρτέμιδος.
> αὔριον ἀλλὰ πάτρη με δεδέξεται, ἐς δὲ σὸν ὄμμα
> πτήσομαι· ἐρρῶσθαι μυρία σ' εὐχόμενος.

Strato *A.P.* 12.226

> πάννυχα μυδαλόεντα πεφυρμένος ὄμματα κλαυθμῶι
> ἄγρυπνον ἀμπαύω θυμὸν ἀδημονίηι,
> ἦ με κατ' οὖν ἐδάμασσεν ἀποζευχθέντος ἑταίρου,
> μοῦνον ἐπεί με λιπὼν εἰς ἰδίην Ἔφεσον

5   χθιζὸς ἔβη Θεόδωρος· ὃς εἰ πάλι μὴ ταχὺς ἔλθοι,
          οὐκέτι μουνολεχεῖς κοίτας ἀνεξόμεθα.

The points of resemblance are: (1) Identity of theme (unendurable separation from the beloved). (2) The scene, Ephesus; though in Rufinus it is the lover who is there, in Strato the beloved. (3) The phrasing: Rufinus δακρύοισι πεφυρμένος, Strato πεφυρμένος ὄμματα κλαυθμῶι; Rufinus οὐκέτι βαστάζω...μουνολεχῆ σεῖο διαζυγίην, Strato οὐκέτι μουνολεχεῖς κοίτας ἀνεξόμεθα.
Of these points the first is negligible, for the theme is commonplace. The second point may be fortuitous coincidence; Ephesus attracted many visitors (*cf.* Peek 697, 970, 1081). In the phrasing the first resemblance may be insignificant, for πεφυρμένος is commonplace in such contexts (see the Commentary); but the second resemblance is not so easily disposed of. The two authors are very much alike here, and they have in common the very rare word μουνολεχής, which both use in the sense 'sleeping without a bed-fellow', contrary to the vernacular, in which it meant 'sleeping always with the same bed-fellow', *i.e.* being a faithful spouse. Mere coincidence cannot be ruled out but seems unlikely. The chances are that one has the other in mind, consciously or subconsciously.

(*b*) Rufinus VII and Strato 12.229

Both epigrams have the same theme, the impermanence of beauty. There is no other particular resemblance between them in thought or expression until the end:

Rufinus   ὡς δὲ τάφον νῦν σε παρερχόμεθα.

Strato   χοὶ θέραπες νῦν σε παρερχόμεθα.

Here, however, the difference is as marked as the similarity, which is limited to common words expressing a common idea, νῦν σε παρερχόμεθα. Where Rufinus has ὡς δὲ τάφον, Strato has the wholly different χοὶ θέραπες. Mere coincidence in the use of the words νῦν σε παρερχόμεθα seems likely here.

(c) Rufinus II and Strato 11.19

It has been maintained that the one is an imitation of the other; but they have nothing in common except the popular theme and the use of a word which is commonplace in such contexts, πυκάʒειν (see the Commentary).

In summary, the evidence of the resemblances between Rufinus I and Strato 12.226 makes it likely, though not certain, that the one was familiar with the other's verse; the question of priority remains to be asked.

It is generally supposed that Strato is the earlier, but the reasons given are of doubtful validity. There is no clear internal evidence either for the absolute date of Strato or for his relation to Rufinus. In metrical technique he differs from the authors of Philip's *Garland*, from Rufinus, and from the *Cycle* (see pp. 37–8 below); and there is nothing in his syntax, vocabulary, or style to make one period preferable to another within the first four centuries A.D.

External sources offer two witnesses: first, Diogenes Laertius, who includes a ποιητὴς ἐπιγραμμάτων in a list of persons named Strato; secondly, the name Capito in an epigram ascribed to Strato (*A.P.* 11.117). The value of these testimonies is questionable.

The date of Diogenes Laertius cannot be defined precisely. He is later than Favorinus (*c.* A.D. 80–150). His upper limit is generally placed in the first half of the third century, not later than the middle part of it, on the ground that such a book as his would not have been written after neo-Platonism had begun to absorb the whole of Greek philosophy. One would welcome a more objective argument; and it is not absolutely certain, though probable enough, that the epigrammatist Strato in Diogenes' list is the same person as the Sardian of the Anthology. We may nevertheless agree that the evidence of Diogenes makes the middle of the third century a likely upper limit for the lifetime of Strato.

The lower limit is much more doubtful. In *A.P.* 11.117 an epigram ascribed to Strato satirises a doctor named Capito, and J. G. Schneider identified this person with Artemidorus Capito,

editor of Hippocrates in the time of Hadrian. This is a very
long shot. The medical scholar who enjoyed the patronage of
the emperor was not a likely target for satire of this kind; and
the assumption that the name of the person satirised in the
epigram is real, not fictitious, should not be allowed to pass
without question.

This matter is large and amorphous, but a few relevant
criteria are worth stating:

(a) In general, satire in *A.P.* XI seems to be more often of
types than of individuals; but the names are presumably real
where one of the following conditions is satisfied: (1) That the
name is ill-suited to the metre: Πωλιανός in 11.228 and Λολλιανός
in 11.274 are metrically awkward; if the persons had been
fictitious, names suitable to the metre would have been chosen.[1]
(2) That the point of the epigram lies in a joke about the name:
Στέφανος φιλοστέφανος in 11.17, Ἀντώνιος ὤνιος in 11.181,
Χίλων λείχων in 11.222, Μάρκος ἄρκος in 11.231, Δαμαγόρας
isopsephic with λοιμός in 11.334, Δράκων δράκων in 11.22.

(b) On the other hand, if the same name recurs frequently
in a wide variety of contexts, it is likely to be fictitious in some,
probably many, of them. It is not probable that Lucillius knew
a poet (11.10), an astrologer (11.164), a miser (11.172), a thief
(11.176), a coward (11.210), and a boxer (11.258) all named
Aulus; or an athlete (11.85), a very small thin man (11.90,
93–4), a rhetorician (11.143), a hunter (11.194), a notoriously
lazy man (11.276–7), and a poet (11.135, 312) all named
Marcus. Roman *praenomina* are indeed few in number, and
Marcus is at least once a true name (11.231); but there are
certain recurrent Greek names which argue rather for types
than persons, and the Roman *praenomina* are probably of the
same sort: *Diophantus* is a very small man in 11.103, a very thin
one in 11.111, an astrologer in 11.114, a ship-master in 11.245,
and a doctor's patient in 11.257. *Heliodorus* is a poet in 11.134,
a bad host in 11.137, a schoolmaster in 11.138, stealer of a
statue in 11.183, and a man who made a bad purchase in

---

[1] In 11.309 the name Θαρσύμαχος may be Θρασύμαχος adapted to the
metre; but the name is so spelt, Θαρσύμαχος, in the heading to Peek 1513.

11.244. *Eutychides* is a poet in 11.133, a thief in 11.175, 177, and a glutton in 11.205, 208.

As for Strato himself, the most striking fact about his lover-names is their large number: 40 occur once each, only 4 twice and only 2 thrice. It is a comfort to hear (12.258) that his epigrams were written not for himself but for others who employed him for this purpose. If this is so, those epigrams which include lover-names probably refer (most if not all of them) to real persons, and the names are likely to be real; fictitious names would have been apt to cause confusion – it would have been necessary for Strato to make sure that a fictitious name was not also the true name of some other person within the circle of his employer's acquaintance (some discarded lover, perhaps).

We now return to our starting-point and ask whether the name Capito in 11.117 is more likely to be real than fictitious; and the answer must take account of the following points:

(*a*) Excepting the Prologue and Epilogue to *A.P.* XII, this is the only non-amatory epigram ascribed to Strato. It is a satirical piece, quite uncharacteristic of Strato both in its subject and in its position in the Anthology, interposed as it is between solid blocks from Nicarchus and Callicter. There is an obvious possibility that the ascription to Strato is false.[1]

(*b*) 11.117 is one of a series of eleven satirical epigrams on physicians; it is unlikely that all, if any, are directed against individuals.

The general conclusion is that *A.P.* 11.117 may not be the work of Strato, and that the name Capito is at least as likely to be fictitious as real. The identification with Artemidorus Capito is risky; it is rather more likely to be wrong than right; it is not reliable evidence for the date of Strato. The upper limit for Rufinus is the end of the fourth century, for Strato probably the middle of the third. The lower limit is not known for either of them,[2] and if one knew the other's epigrams we have not yet any useful evidence about priority.

[1] *Cf.* L. Schmidt in *RE* 1.2382; Budé vol. x 115 n. 2.

[2] Martial is no help. Some popular themes are common to Martial and Rufinus, but no epigram by the one is at all like any epigram by the other. Boas (*l.c.*) gives sufficient answer to Sakolowski on this point.

THE METRICAL TECHNIQUE OF RUFINUS

The metrical technique of Rufinus will now be examined, in the hope that it may indicate at least whether he lived relatively early or relatively late within the period A.D. 50–400. It would be particularly interesting if his technique were strikingly similar to that of the *Cycle* of Agathias at the one extreme or that of the *Garland* of Philip at the other.

Among the numerous points which have been considered, a few are selected as appearing likelier than most to differentiate one period from another.

I PROPAROXYTONE HEXAMETER-ENDS

(1) The *Cycle* avoids ending the hexameter with a trisyllabic proparoxytone word. There are only 39 exceptions to the rule in 1,138 lines = 3·4 %.

(2) Accent on the last syllable of the fifth dactyl is indeed avoided in the *Cycle* more generally: there are only 7 examples of proparoxytone quadrisyllables at line-end, 5 of proparoxytone pentasyllables, and 21 of proparoxytone pentasyllabic word-groups (*e.g.* πλεξαμένη δέ, γυιοβόρον γάρ). ἠέρτημαι in Paulus 5.230.7 is a special case.

(3) Rufinus observes no such law. He has 12 trisyllabic proparoxytones at line-end,[1] = 12 %, and altogether 32 of 97 lines end with an accent on the last syllable of the fifth dactyl.[2]

(4) Rufinus' proportion of trisyllabic proparoxytones at line-end is about the random standard: Meleager has 13 %, Philip 14 %, Palladas 13.3 %.

---

[1] Including the word-groups τίνος σε and βάλοι δέ, to which the only parallels in the Cycle are φίλοις τε and κύβωι τε.

[2] Not counting μαρμαίροντα and εἰλίσσοντο, which resemble Paulus' ἠέρτημαι.

II   CAESURA IN THE HEXAMETER

(1) In the *Cycle* all lines have caesura in the third foot; feminine (65 %) is nearly twice as common as masculine (35 %).

(2) This penthemimeral caesura is followed by bucolic caesura in 63 % of 1,134 lines: feminine + bucolic caesura with pause in 221 lines, without pause in 179, = 400; masculine + bucolic caesura with pause in 211 lines, without pause in 102, = 313.

(3) Where the main caesura is not followed by bucolic caesura, lines with feminine caesura differ from lines with masculine caesura in two respects:

(*a*) Following feminine caesura, there is a marked preference for word-division after the fifth trochee (214) rather than after the fifth long (47) or the fifth dactyl (76). Following masculine caesura there is no preference for word-division after the fifth trochee (43); division after the fifth dactyl is almost as common (37); but

(*b*) following masculine caesura, word-division after the fifth long is almost excluded (only in *A.P.* 6.12.1, 7.576.1, 9.661.5, *Plan.* 37.3).

(4) There are four anomalous lines (not included in the above count): two with word-division after the fourth trochee (Agathias 7.568.1 and 7), one with caesura after the fourth *biceps* (Barbucallus *Plan.* 38.3), and one with spondaic fifth foot including word-division after the fifth long (Agathias *Plan.* 331.1).

(5) Rufinus differs in several respects:

(*a*) He does not share the *Cycle*'s marked preference for feminine caesura; he has 54 feminine, 46 masculine.

(*b*) He does not avoid word-division after the fifth long in lines with masculine caesura; he has three in 100 lines, whereas the *Cycle* has only 4 in 1,134.

(*c*) Where feminine caesura is not followed by bucolic caesura, he shows no preference for word-division after the fifth trochee, dividing there in ten examples but not in sixteen others.

III OXYTONE PENTAMETER-ENDS

(1) It is a rule of the *Cycle* that an accented syllable should not stand at the end of the pentameter. The rule is broken in only 9 of 1,138 lines (monosyllable, Barbucallus *Plan.* 219.2; disyllables, Cometas 5.265.2, Leontius 7.579.4, Julianus 9.739.2, Macedonius 5.238.6, Paulus 5.279.6; trisyllables, Agathias 5.280.4, Macedonius 10.71.2; quadrisyllable, Irenaeus 5.253.2).

(2) Rufinus has a very low percentage, 2 accented ends in 99; but in this respect he is not more like the *Cycle* than some earlier poets. The random-range may be given by Theognis (22 % accented ends) and Callimachus (17 % in the epigrams, 18.3 % in *Lav. Pall.*). Avoidance of accented ends is seen earliest in Antipater of Sidon (1.5 %), whose example is followed by most of Philip's authors; of the 1,887 pentameters assembled in *The Garland of Philip*, only 73 end in accented syllables, and a high proportion of the exceptions are in two authors, Philodemus (13 %) and Crinagoras (7.6 %). Antipater of Thessalonica (3 %) and Philip (1 %) very seldom break the law, and there are no exceptions in Bianor or Argentarius. Lucillius and Nicarchus (8.3 %), Strato (over 9 %) and Palladas (9 %) admit such ends quite freely, Gregory of Nazianzus (1.5 %) almost excludes them.

IV LONG AND LENGTHENED SYLLABLES BEFORE THE PENTAMETER-CAESURA

(1) It is a general rule in the *Cycle* that the syllable preceding the median caesura in the pentameter should be, or contain, a long vowel or diphthong. Exceptions to the rule amount to only about 5 %. Authors in Philip's *Garland* are still stricter: of 1,887 pentameters, only 3 % break the rule (Crinagoras, with 13 exceptions in 144 lines, is the only Philippan author whose practice is random). Philodemus has 1 exception in 93 lines; there is no exception in Apollonides (78 lines), Bianor (61) or Philip (204). A random sample, if Theognis may be assumed to give one, offers 15.5 % lengthened, as opposed to long, syllables.

Callimachus and Leonidas, each with 12%, are presumably within the random range. Antipater of Sidon, with 5.8%, is the earliest to show a preference for naturally long syllables in this position.

(2) Rufinus has no apparent preference: 10% of his pentameters are exceptions to the rule. Strato has 8% exceptions, Lucillius and Nicarchus 9%, Palladas nearly 10%.

V HIATUS, ELISION, 'BREVIS IN LONGO', AND LENGTHENING OF SHORT VOWELS, IN MID-PENTAMETER

(1) Hiatus in mid-pentameter is very rare at all times: 'Demodocus' *A.P.* 11.237.2, Theognis 478 (emendable), 'Simonides' *A.P.* 7.251.2, anon. 12.130.4 = *HE* 3765, Archias 6.181.6 = *PG* 3619 (emendable), Dionysius Sophistes 5.81.2 (combined with *brevis in longo*), Lucillius 11.313.4, Nicarchus 11.74.10, Diogenes Laertius 7.133.4, Palladas 7.687.2 and (combined with *brevis in longo*) 10.44.4; and a number of undatable epigrams of uncertain authorship or anonymous, *inc. auct. A.P.* 9.35.2, 7.699.8 = *PG* 3509 (emendable), 7.134.2, 9.191.4, 9.384.6 and 8, 11.151.2, 11.339.2; in the *Cycle*, only Barbucallus 9.425.2 κεῖμαι, | ἄ. Sophronius 7.679.4 and 8. The large collection of epigrams in Peek's *Griechische Vers-Inschriften* has only one early example, 339.2 βελτίστα, | ἁ δὲ (Rhodian Peraea, IV B.C., *stoichedon*), and only four others earlier than the Christian era (1138.1, 1261.4, 1417.2, 1710.2, all II B.C.); two examples are dated I A.D. and five I–II A.D.; from III to IV A.D. there are nearly forty examples.[1]

---

[1] The list of examples from Theognis and the Anthology has 21 items (not counting Rufinus); 6 of them have the genitive -ου before the caesura, as in Simonides *l.c.* θανάτου | ἀμφ-. Those who think Demodocus *l.c.* supposititious and Theognis *l.c.* corrupt can properly deny that there is any example earlier than Peek 339.2, or any literary example before the Christian era except anon. *A.P.* 12.130.4 (a couple of others being easily emended); they may therefore be justified in reading θανάτοι' (Ahrens) in Simonides *l.c.* if that epigram comes from the fifth century. The only examples of this elision known to me in elegiac verse of early date are Peek 145 (Athens, VI B.C.) ὁδοῖ' ἀγαθοῦ, 917.1 (Amorgos, IV B.C.) [—∪ ἀ]ποφθιμένοι' | ἐνθάδε Κα[λλιμάχου, and 1178 (Rhodian Peraea, II

Rufinus v 4 offers, as it stands, an example of hiatus at mid-pentameter, but it is so easily emendable that it should be withdrawn from the list (see the Commentary).

(2) Elision of δέ and τε appears commonly, of γε, με, and σε rarely, at mid-pentameter in the two *Garlands* and earlier elegiac poetry. Later authors seldom allow these elisions: Rufinus has no example; Lucillius, Nicarchus, and Strato together have only 15 examples in 590 lines; Palladas has 3 in 290, the *Cycle* 12 in 1,138. Elision of longer words is not common. There are 20 examples in Theognis, 18 in all other elegiac poetry from Archilochus to Antimachus, 35 in *HE*, of which 24 are in Asclepiades, Callimachus, Leonidas, Meleager and Posidippus; only 10 examples in *PG*. Thereafter it is a rare phenomenon: no examples in Rufinus, Palladas, or the *Cycle*. Strato has three examples, Lucillius one, Nicarchus two. There are not many in inscriptional epigrams: earliest is Peek 1223.2, VI B.C., οἴκτιρ' | ὅς; there are 8 or 9 examples from IV B.C., 8 from III–II B.C., 3 from I B.C.; from I to IV A.D., less than 20 examples.

(3) *Brevis in longo* before the pentameter-caesura is very rare: Theognis 2 and 1232; Antipater of Sidon *A.P.* 7.745.4 and 7.218.10 = *HE* 289 and 329, both probably corrupt; the only others in *HE* are Phaedimus 6.271.6 = 2906 and anon. 7.298.6 = 3869, both probably corrupt; there is no example in *PG* (Glaucus 9.775.2 = 3874 is certainly corrupt). Other examples are Dionysius Sophistes 5.81.2 (combined with hiatus), Lucianus 9.120.2, 11.410.6, 11.431.2, 11.435.2, Strato 12.216.2, Palladas 6.85.2 and (combined with hiatus) 10.44.4, anon. 7.349.2, 9.148.2, 9.612.2, *Plan.* 19.2, 53.2. There is no example in Rufinus, Lucillius, Nicarchus or the *Cycle*. The inscriptions have one early example, Peek 1888.4 (IV B.C.) 'Α]ρ[ι]σ[τ]όκρ[-ιτ]ον | ὤλεσε, and two others earlier than the Christian era, 1138.8 (II B.C.) and 1700.6 (I B.C.); thereafter only one example before II A.D., but 32 from II to IV A.D.

B.C.) ἀντιθέοιο ἀλόχου. *Cf.* also 'Simonides' 8.11, *IEG* II 115 West, a line ending καὶ βιότου ὀλίγος, where Camerarius conjectured βιότοι' ὀλίγος, and Archilochus *fr.* 120. 1.

(4) Lengthening of final short vowels at mid-pentameter is a peculiarity almost confined to the Hellenistic poets: (a) Lengthening by initial mute + liquid consonants: Theognis 346 τάμᾱ | χρήματ', Leonidas *A.P.* 7.506.10 = *HE* 2368, Mnasalces 6.264.2 = *HE* 2622, 'Theocritus' *Id.* 8.54, Palladas 9.174.10, anon. 11.425.2. The only example in Peek is of early date, 891.2 (IV B.C.) τοῦτ̄ο | πλεῖστον. Short vowel before mid-pentameter followed by βλ-, γλ-, γν-, μν-, is avoided in all periods; Callimachus *A.P.* 6.310.2 = *HE* 1176 δε̄ | Γλαῦκος, Macedonius *Plan.* 51.2 τῆιδε̄ | μνάματος. (b) Lengthening by combinations other than mute + liquid: before 3, Archelaus II ii p. 82 Diehl, Leonidas *A.P.* 6.221.6 = *HE* 2296, Menecrates 9.390.4 = *HE* 2592, Theaetetus *ap.* Diog. Laert. 4.25 = *HE* 3351; Peek 164.2 ἔτ]ῑ 3ῶσαν, if the restoration is correct. Before other combinations: Leonidas 7.408.2 = *HE* 2326 ἐγείρητε | σφῆκ', Callimachus 9.566.4 = *HE* 1308 φησὶ | σκληρά, Meleager 7.195.8 = *HE* 4065 στόμασι | σχι3ο- (this and the preceding could be eliminated by reading φησίν, στόμασιν, but the use of paragogic *nu* to assist lengthening in mid-pentameter is not common), Mnasalces 6.9.4 = *HE* 2610 ὀλοὰ | ξείνια, Agathias *Plan.* 36.4 γραφίδι | στήσομεν, Peek 1334.2 (III A.D.) μάθε | στάς.

Except Theognis *l.c.*, there is no example of any of these types in pre-Alexandrian elegiacs; there is none in the *Garland* of Philip; Peek's inscriptions have only the three examples quoted.

(5) There is no example in literature of a pentameter lacking a median caesura, as in Peek 217.2 (early V B.C.) ἀνώ-|ρως.

VI ELISION

(1) It is a general rule in the *Cycle* that elision is freely admitted only in particles, pronouns (especially cases of ὅδε; τοῦτο, ταῦτα), prepositions, certain conjunctions, and a few common adverbs (especially ἐνθάδε, ἔτι, τότε). Nouns are not as a rule elided, nor are verbs (except ἐστί, and ἴδε in the phrase ἴδ' ὡς) or adjectives (except ὅσα, πάντα, πολλά).

INTRODUCTION

The *Cycle* is indeed very strict in this matter. Elided nouns appear in only three places: Macedonius 6.83.2 χεῖρ', Theaetetus Scholasticus *Plan.* 221.8 δαίμον' and Leontius *Plan.* 288.1 οὔνομ'; in Julianus 7.561.1 ἀνέρα τίκτεν should be read. The only elided adjective (apart from ὅσα, πάντα, πολλά) is in Agathias 11.379.7 μέγ'. Elided verbs appear only in Paulus 5.244.7 μίμν', Macedonius 11.366.2 ἤθελ', Barbucallus 9.426.5 γράψατ', 9.427.6 χαίρετ' (twice), Agathias 11.64.4 νήχετ' (the only elided -αι in the *Cycle*) and 7.568.4 ἠγάγετ' (the only elided quadrisyllable in the *Cycle*, not reckoning οὐδέ ποτ').

(2) Moreover the *Cycle* is very sparing of elision even in the common categories, except of ἀλλά (47) and δέ (221): τε 23, οὐδέ μηδέ οὔτε μήτε 29, ἀντί 8, ἀπό 13, ἀνά 2, ἀμφί 1, διά 2, ἐπί 27, κατά 7, μετά 5, παρά 11, ὑπό 11, με 11, σε 1, γε 2, ὅτε ποτέ τότε 10, ἔτι 1, ἄρα 7, ὅδε 14, τοῦτο ταῦτα 5, πάντα 3, ἔνθα 1, δεῦρο 2, εὔτε 2, ἴδε ὅσσα τῆλε τινά 1 each; of trisyllables, only οὔνεκα εἴνεκα 3, ἄλλοθι αὐτόθι ἐνθάδε μηκέτι 1 each.

(3) The *Cycle* never allows elision at the main caesura, whether masculine or feminine, in the hexameter.

(4) Avoidance of elision in nouns, adjectives, and verbs is a characteristic of elegiac verse from the earliest period onwards. Theognis has only 18 elided verb-forms (not reckoning εἰμί, ἐστί) in 1,389 lines, and only 31 elided nouns or adjectives (not reckoning Κύρνε, πάντα, πολλά). The ratio of all such elisions (of nouns, adjectives, and verbs) to the total of lines in Callimachus' epigrams is 5 %, in Antipater of Sidon 2 %, in Argentarius less than 3 %, in Antipater of Thessalonica 2.7 %, in Philodemus 3.2 %, in Antiphilus 1.9 %, in Philip 5 %. A few of the Hellenistic epigrammatists indicate what may be the random-range: Asclepiades 14 %, Leonidas 11 %, Dioscorides and Meleager each about 8 %. Of the later authors, Lucillius and Nicarchus show about 4·2 %, Strato 4·3 %; Palladas, like the *Cycle*, almost excludes such elisions (5 examples in 580 lines).

(5) Rufinus, like Antipater of Sidon, Palladas, and the *Cycle*, is very strict in this matter: he has only one elided verb and two nouns in 199 lines (xvii 4 φεύγετ', xxv 2 Μαιονίδ', xxxv 1 ὄμματ'). He has one elision which does not occur elsewhere in

34

elegiac verse, of σά in 1 3. He has no elision at the main caesura in either the hexameter or the pentameter.

VII EPIC CORREPTION[1]

(1) The *Cycle* freely admits correption only of -μαι, -εαι and -ται in verb-forms, and these only in words of three, four, or five syllables at the bucolic caesura (47 examples) or of three syllables at the end of the first (4) and fifth (14) dactyl in the hexameter and of the first dactyl in either half of the pentameter (16, 28).

(2) Correption of vowels or diphthongs other than -μαι, -εαι and -ται in these positions is rare: in words of three or more syllables, Agathias *A.P.* 7.551.1, 10.69.5, Julianus 9.481.3, Leontius 7.579.2, Paulus 5.232.8, 7.609.4; in words of less than three syllables, Agathias 5.269.3, 5.273.7, 6.80.3, 7.220.3, 10.66.1, Eratosthenes 5.277.1, Marianus *Plan.* 201.9, Paulus 6.64.7, 7.307.1, all at the bucolic caesura, Synesius *Plan.* 267.5 at the first dactyl.

(3) ἤ or ἡ is shortened at the end of the third dactyl in Agathias 5.289.1, 7.76.5, 11.354.5, Arabius 9.667.5, *Plan.* 144.1; and at the end of the dactyl following the pentameter-caesura in Agathias 11.354.14.

(4) Correption of the first short of the dactyl is rare (35 examples).

(5) Correption at the feminine caesura in the hexameter is not allowed.

(6) Rufinus is in all respects except one indistinguishable from the *Cycle*: he has 15 correptions in 199 lines, about the same proportion as in the *Cycle*; 9 are of verbal -μαι or -ται at the bucolic caesura or at the end of the first dactyl, 4 are of other vowels or diphthongs at the bucolic caesura. Correption of the first short of the dactyl occurs only once (XI 4 λευκῆι). But correption at the feminine caesura, excluded by the *Cycle*, appears once in Rufinus (XXXVII 3 λευκαί σοῖ).

---

[1] Not counting correption of καί, which is very common, or of μοι, σοι, and τοι, which is rare in elegiac verse.

(7) The ratio of number of corruptions to number of lines is about 15 % in Theognis, 11 % in Leonidas, 16 % in Crinagoras; these presumably indicate the random-range. Callimachus has only 4 examples in the 274 lines of his epigrams; Antipater of Sidon (3·6 %) and Meleager (3·3 %) admit corruption sparingly; Argentarius is very strict, with only 8 examples, all of verbal -μαι or -ται at the bucolic caesura or ends of first dactyls, in 204 lines; Philip has only 6 examples in 408 lines. Lucillius and Nicarchus revert to more or less random standards (8.3 %). Strato and Palladas are fairly conservative (each 5.7 %, mostly of the types which are freely admitted by the *Cycle*).

VIII HIATUS[1]

If, as seems probable,[2] Rufinus xxii 5 is corrupt, the only hiatus in his epigrams is xii 7 ὑάλωι ἴσος. His versification appears in this respect highly conservative in comparison with other epigrammatists of the first six centuries A.D.:

Lucillius and Nicarchus: N. 11.114.1, Λ. 11.164.2 ὁ ἀστρολόγος, Λ. 11.276.1 ὁ ἀργός, N. 11.251.3 τὸ ἐνοίκιον, N. 11.96.3 ὦ ἐλεειναί, Λ. 11.132.5 ὦ ὕπατε Ζεῦ, Λ. 11.107.3 Τιτυῶι ἐναλίγκιος, 11.253.3 ἢ ἀπό, N. 11.241.3 σε ἔδει, Λ. 11.259.1 'Ερασίστρατε ἄλλο.

Callicter: 11.118.1 ἥψατο ἀλλά.

Strato: 12.3.3 λάλου ὀνόμαζε, 12.8.1 παῖδα ἐπανθ-, 12.8.7 καὶ οἴκαδ', 12.209.3 πρὸ ἔργων, 12.239.1 ἀντία ἕξεις (*s.v.l.*), 12.246.3 ἀποστείχει ὁ δ', 12.246.1 φιλεῖ οὐκ.

Palladas: 7.681.3 τροχαλώτερε ἐκ, 9.173.5 τὰ ἑλώρια, 9.174.8 τὸ ἔθος, 9.394.2 τὸ ἔχειν, 9.393.3 τὸ ἀγνόν, 10.53.4 εἰ ὁ, 10.55.1 μὴ ὑπακούειν, 10.79.1 γεννώμεθα ἦμαρ, 9.174.12 ὅλου ἔτεος.

The Cycle: Paulus 5.241.7, 5.275.9, 6.57.6, 6.75.1 ὦι or ὅι ἔπι, Agathias 10.64.2 πῇ ἔβαν, Paulus 5.258.1 ἢ ὁπός, Arabius *Plan.* 148.4 ἢ ἀπό, Barbucallus 9.425.4 φεῦ ἀπό, Agathias 7.76.1 τοῦ εἵνεκα, 5.282.1 τανᾶου ἔπι, 5.280.5 τὰ ὅμοια, 6.79.5 τὸ ἐπαύλιον, 11.365.7 τὸ ἀρούριον. Hiatus after καί and σοι (except in correption) is extremely rare: Agathias 11.376.9 ἢ σοὶ ἤ, Cometas 9.597.8 καὶ ὅλος. Macedonius 10.70.3 has εὖ οἶδα.

---

[1] Not counting examples in correption or (see v above) in mid-pentameter or before the pronoun οἱ. On hiatus in *HE* and *PG*, see *The Garland of Philip* i.xl–xli.

[2] See the Commentary.

IX PAUSE AT END OF DISTICH

In Rufinus the sense is actually or potentially complete at the end of all distichs except xxiv 1–2, where the pentameter ends a clause but the sentence is not potentially complete. Carry-over without any pause at all does not occur. In the *Cycle* about 90 % of distichs end with the sense actually or potentially complete; within the remaining 10 % carry-over without any pause at all is very rare (less than 20 examples in 1,136 distichs). In Palladas carry-over without pause occurs only twice (9.502.2–3, 10.50.6–7); in Strato only once (12.226.4–5); in Lucillius and Nicarchus never.

X COMPARISON WITH THE 'GARLAND' OF PHILIP

There is no significant difference in metrical technique between Rufinus and an ordinary author in Philip's *Garland* such as Apollonides, Argentarius, Philodemus, or Philip himself. Any feature in which he differs from one, therein he agrees with another. He differs from Philip, for example, in freely allowing the lengthening of short syllables by position at mid-penta-meter, but in this respect he resembles Antiphilus (6 %) and is less free than Antiphanes (6 examples in 29 lines). He differs from Philodemus in the proportion of accented pentameter-ends (2 %–13 %), but in this respect he is very like Philip (1 %). In common with all Philippan authors he freely admits pro-paroxytone hexameter-ends. There is, in brief, no feature of his versification which is not characteristic of one or more of the *Garland*-authors.

XI COMPARISON WITH STRATO

There are striking differences between Rufinus and Strato:

(*a*) Elision, which in Rufinus is relatively rare and highly conventional in types, is more or less indiscriminate in Strato, who is one of the few epigrammatists who have no prejudice against eliding nouns and verbs (22 examples in 468 lines; Rufinus has 3 in 199).

4   37

(*b*) Strato ends the pentameter with an accented syllable 22 times in 234 chances, Rufinus only twice in 100.

(*c*) Strato allows elision at mid-pentameter not only of δέ and τε but also of longer words (12.197.2 ἀκμάζοντ᾽, 12.247.2 θεράποντ᾽, 12.16.4 τοιάνδ᾽) and once allows *brevis in longo* (12.216.2 ἐχθές | οὐδέν). Rufinus has nothing of the kind.

(*d*) Strato allows elision at the main caesura in the hexameter (12.8.5, 12.13.1, 12.247.1), Rufinus does not.

(*e*) Strato twice (12.188.1, 12.245.3) allows word-division after the fourth trochee and six times (12.6.1, 12.8.3, 12.180.1, 12.194.3, 12.208.7, 12.218.3) admits words of the shape ∪ – – before the bucolic caesura. Rufinus has two examples of the latter type but none of the former.

(*f*) Strato admits hiatus of types which are alien to the style and technique of Rufinus (see VIII above).

(*g*) Strato allows hephthemimeral caesura. There is no example of this in Rufinus (or in the *Cycle*).

XII COMPARISON WITH PALLADAS

Palladas and Rufinus are alike in some respects:

(*a*) Both are sparing of elision, especially of nouns, adjectives and verbs. The only anomalous elision in Palladas is 10.88.1, where μοῖρ᾽ stands at the end of the fourth foot.

(*b*) Both are sparing of correption, and neither is far from the strict rules of the *Cycle* (see VII above); the only examples alien to the *Cycle*-rules in Palladas are 10.49.3 μὴ ἔχοντα, where μὴ σχόντα could be read, 11.381.1 δυῶ ὥρας, 11.293.1 μοῖ at the feminine caesura (like σοι in Rufinus XXXVII 3).

(*c*) Both freely allow the lengthening of short syllables by position at mid-pentameter.

In other respects they differ:

(i) Palladas admits hiatus of types which are alien to the style and technique of Rufinus (see VIII above).

(ii) Palladas has four examples of word-division at the fourth trochee (9.6.1, 11.300.1, 11.385.1, 11.387.1), one of *brevis in longo* at the masculine caesura (11.340.1), and two of hephthemimeral caesura (9.503.1, 10.56.5). None of these things occurs in Rufinus.

(iii) Palladas admits *brevis in longo* at the pentameter-caesura in 6.85.2 and again, accompanied by hiatus, in 10.44.4; in 9.174.10 a short final vowel is lengthened by position in mid-pentameter, μηνῖ | πρίν. Rufinus has none of these things.

(iv) Palladas' prosody is irregular in 9.168.1 μηνῖν, 9.169.5 πρῖν, 9.173.1, 7 κατᾱρα, 9.378.4 τάλᾰς, 10.34.1 μερίμνᾱ, 10.44.1, 2 φρᾱτερ, 10.51.4 ἄγᾰν, 11.280.3 φονέᾱς, 11.387.2 ἀριστῶμεν. Rufinus has ἐρῐσασα, ἐκδέδῠκας, ἡρᾰσάμην and probably κέκρᾰγεν.

XIII COMPARISON WITH THE 'CYCLE' OF AGATHIAS

Rufinus is clearly differentiated from the *Cycle* by his free admission of proparoxytone hexameter-ends; by his indifference to the rule that the syllable preceding the pentameter-caesura should be (or include) a long vowel or a diphthong; by his example of correction of the syllable preceding the feminine caesura in the hexameter; and by several minor features noted above.

XIV GENERAL CONCLUSIONS

(1) That, if Rufinus had been preserved as an author in the *Garland* of Philip, the tradition could not have been challenged on any point of metrical technique.
(2) That Rufinus and Strato observe very different rules of versification.
(3) That Rufinus and Palladas have much in common, but Palladas allows himself certain liberties of which there is no trace in Rufinus.
(4) That, if Rufinus had been preserved as a *Cycle*-author, the differences in his technique would have proved that the tradition was in error, or at least that Rufinus was a solitary non-conformist in that company.

PROSODY

The enquiry has not so far brought to light any clear indication of the lower date-limit for the life of Rufinus. He is indeed close to the *Garland* of Philip in metrical technique; but there remain certain points of prosody to be considered, and these, taken together, seem not to favour a relatively early date.

There are four false quantities in the text of Rufinus which have been called tokens of *infima Graecitas*.

(1) XXXI 2 κέκρᾱγεν. The change to κέκρᾱγ' is easy and may be right, but it is not to be accepted without more ado. Elision of verb-endings is very rare in Rufinus as in other authors (see p. 34 above); moreover, words of this shape, – – ∪, where the last is a short vowel, are never elided in 2,276 lines of the *Cycle*, and the 199 lines of Rufinus have no other example. There is therefore reason to hesitate before introducing this feature into his text by way of conjecture.

The error may be rather of accidence than of prosody. The perfect tense of κράζω is not very commonly used,[1] and Rufinus may have thought that as the aorist was ἔκρᾱγεν[2] the perfect should be κέκρᾱγεν.

If there were no comparable error in Rufinus, it would be prudent to accept κέκρᾱγ'; but it is not alone.

(2) XXVII 6 ἐκδέδῠκας. The perfect active of δύω is elsewhere always δέδῡκα. There is indeed some variation of quantity in the stem of the verb, but only where δυ- is followed by a vowel.

Here again the error may be rather of accidence than of prosody: the analogy of θύω τέθῠκα may have led Rufinus to conjugate δύω δέδῠκα. But δέδῠκα is a good deal commoner in use than κέκραγα, and it looks as though Rufinus cannot be acquitted of the charge of gross mispronunciation of a common word.

The bearing of this on the question of his date remains

---

[1] They pronounced it properly, however, in Panticapaeum in the second or first century B.C. (Peek 845.7); and so did Babrius (3.10, 5.6).

[2] Conjectured here by Veitch (*Greek Verbs* 387) and again by Stadtmüller; but the tense is unsuitable.

doubtful. It is tenable that δέδυκα in Rufinus is not more appalling than the future tense-form ἀναδράμεται in a writer of the first half of the first century A.D., Philip of Thessalonica (9.575.4 = *PG* 3012); everybody knew that the proper form was δραμεῖται, and it is hard to think of any justification for this eccentricity. The same author was capable of putting ἔστᾰσε where ἔστησε was required (9.708.6 = *PG* 3020). Antipater of Thessalonica (9.309.3 = *PG* 421), Philip (9.262.4 = *PG* 2830), and Diogenes Laertius (*A.P.* 7.88.3) all scan ἥμῦσα, for ἥμῡσα, an error similar in principle to δέδυκα in Rufinus.

(3) III 3 ἐρῐσασα. ἐρῐσασα, for ἐρείσασα, is an extraordinary error. There is no serious doubt about the reading: ἐρείδειν is exactly the right verb, and such substitutes as ἐρύσασα (Planudes), ἐπιφῦσα (Bury), ἐφίσασα or ἐπιθεῖσα (Stadtmüller) are obviously unacceptable. Hesychius has the entries ἐριδόμενος, ἐρίδων, ἐρίσει, but these must have been mis-spellings in his sources, ι for ει as often, for there never was a verb ἐρῐδω, ἤρῐσα in Greek.

Some of the earlier editors found a parallel for ἐρῐσασα in δανῐσας, for δανείσας, in Lucillius 11.309.3, *Lyr. Adesp.* 37.27 Powell; but δανίσας may be referred to δανίζειν, as proper a formation from δάνος as ἀνθίζειν from ἄνθος or μελίζειν from μέλος. Nor is the form φθονέσω,[1] for φθονήσω, relevant to the shortening of a long stem-vowel.

(4) XVIII 1: the context requires 'vowed', ἠρᾱσάμην, not 'loved', ἠρᾰσάμην. This is an equally gross error.

That a man may write fluently and in other respects correctly and yet have no ear for quantity is not extraordinary. Gregory of Nazianzus in the fourth century composes interminably and apparently without effort, including in his verse such monsters as λῦσε πᾱσης πᾱσι μάστῐγες Βῑθῡνοί πῐμελή δρᾱσας ἐτῑνάχθην κᾱρες Σῐσύφου μαρτύρομαι ὄμνῡμι λῑτάζομαι λῑτή. Ausonius in the same century knows Greek well, but is still capable of scanning *Phĭdiae solĭcismus* ἀκίνδῠνος Θουκῠδίδου πενῑη ψῠχρά. What seems more surprising is that a generally

---

[1] A quite common type: Peek 1474.2 (I A.D.) ποθέσας, 1576.6 (I–II A.D.) στερέσας, 1905.9 (III A.D.) πονέσας.

correct composer should be capable of very rare but very gross blunders; yet there are some parallels which warn us against using ἐρῑσασα and ἠρᾱσάμην as reliable evidence for a very late date.

(a) In the middle of the second century B.C. Antipater of Sidon (who is nothing if not a *doctus poeta*) scanned εὔμᾰρις (7.413.4 = *HE* 651): this word, being the name of a common object, must have been familiar in conversation, however rare in literature – a foreign word, no doubt, but the Sidonian presumably heard it often enough, and should have known, as Aeschylus (*Pers.* 660), Euripides (*Or.* 1370), and Lycophron (855) knew, that it was pronounced εὔμᾱρις. Still more extraordinary is the same author's false quantity in a very common place-name, 7.81.3 = *HE* 420 Μιτυλᾱνᾰ.

(b) In the middle of the first century B.C. Antipater of Thessalonica scanned πάπῡρος (6.249.2 = *PG* 314). If we had no better evidence for the prosody of this word than the *Anacreontea* (30.5), we should not at once condemn Antipater, especially as some ancient lexicographer[1] said that πάπῡρος was Attic, πάπῡρος common Greek. But it is certain that Antipater's Italian friends said *papȳrus*, as Catullus and Ovid do, and this must have been the quantity in contemporary Greek too.

(c) In the first half of the first century A.D. Philip of Thessalonica, a well-read and eloquent Greek, made a single inexplicable error in a stem-quantity, μιλτοφῠρῆ for μιλτοφῡρῆ (6.103.5 = *PG* 2753).

(d) In the second century A.D. Ammonius pronounces ὁμῑλία twice in one line (9.753.6), Lucianus has Ἀκίνδῠνος (11.429.1), and somebody should have warned the emperor Trajan against ῥῖνα (11.418.1).

(e) In the fourth century Palladas scans ἀριστῶμεν (11.387.2), an astonishing lapse, ἔχθρᾱν (11.340.2), and φρᾰτερ twice in one epigram (10.44).

---

[1] Preserved in Moeris p. 311. Moeris copies out of earlier books without naming his sources. One of these must have had some reason for saying that πάπῡρος was Attic, but we do not know what it was.

Plainly ἐρῐσασα, ἡρᾱσάμην, and ἐκδέδῠκας in Rufinus are not valid evidence for a very late date; there is no case whatsoever against a date in the fourth century A.D., and no need to go so far forward as that.

A curious point about the prosody of Rufinus is that he twice scans πρὄξ- before a verb-stem (v 7, vii 1). This is extremely rare in the Anthology. There is no example in *HE*, *PG*, or the *Cycle*. Lucillius has πρὄξβη (11.86.4) and Palladas has πρὄξθηκας (9.487.1). The phenomenon is rare in the inscriptions: Peek 1752.1 (III–II B.C.) προελίμπανεν, not required by metre but so spelt, and the same is true of 380a2 (II–III A.D.) προελόντε, 819.7 (III A.D.) and 1556.4 προέπεμψε, but in 819.9 προέπεμψαν and 1111.1 (II–III A.D.) προέκρινα stand at the end of the line.

SYNTAX

There is one point in the syntax of Rufinus which some have called a token of *infima Graecitas*: xiv 5 ὅταν ἐστὶν for ὅταν ἦι. Jacobs' change to ὅταν ἦι τις has found much favour.

ὅταν with the indicative is uniformly offered by the manuscripts in Hom. *Od.* 10.410–12 ὅτ' ἄν... σκαίρουσιν and 24.88–9 ὅτε κεν... ζώννυνταί τε νέοι καὶ ἐπεντύνονται ἄεθλα, where change of the text is possible (σκαίρωσιν, ἐπεντύνωνται), and in *Il.* 12.41–2 ὅτ' ἄν... στέρεται, where change is not possible. The construction is offered in Polybius 4.32.5 ὅταν... ἦσαν, and in Strabo 12.3.27 ὅταν δείκνυται (-ύηται conj. Corais).

In an Alexandrian poet this construction might reasonably be explained by reference to a rare Homeric precedent; in Rufinus it more probably reflects vernacular use. It is not a good argument for a date later than the first century A.D. The construction occurs in the Septuagint, in the New Testament, and in inscriptions of the early Christian era; see Arndt and Gingrich, *A Greek–English Lexicon of the New Testament and other Early Christian Literature* (Cambridge & Chicago 1957) 592, with bibliography and examples.

Nor is there any substance in the claim that evidence for a late date is to be found in xxxiii 6 κἂν ὑμεῖς πείσατε τὴν

Ῥοδόπην. The use of κἄν = *saltem* is common in the early centuries A.D.: *e.g.* Philostratus *epist. amat.* 54 (28) εἰ κἀμὲ φεύγεις, ὑπόδεξαι κἂν τὰ ῥόδα, 59 (62) κἂν τοῦτ' αὐτὸ μηνύσατε, 61 (64) κἂν μήνυσον ('you might at least inform me...'); often in Achilles Tatius, *e.g.* 7.5.1 κἂν βλέπων, 7.5.3 κἂν τὴν κεφαλήν; anon. *A.P.* 5.304.2. The sense in Rufinus is 'do you at least (as I have failed to do) persuade her'. The idiom is vernacular, not poetical. In 'Theocritus' 23.41, κἂν νεκρῶι χάρισαι τὰ σὰ χείλεα, κἄν = *etiam*, not *saltem*.

VOCABULARY

There has not yet appeared any evidence to indicate, let alone prove, that any particular date for Rufinus should be preferred within the limits of A.D. 50 and 400. It remains to consider certain items in his vocabulary.

There are several words which point to a period later than the *Garland* of Philip, *e.g.* βαστάζω = *endure*, μετέωρος = *haughty*, φαντασία = *appearance* (what somebody 'looks like'); and there are a few words which, if our information were fuller, would perhaps fix his date very late within the limits.

(1) σοβαρός. Rufinus has this adjective in five places, v 1 τῶν σοβαρῶν, v 3 σοβαρόν τε φρύαγμα, ιχ 4 σοβαρῶν ταρσῶν, xxxiii 2 σοβαραῖς ὀφρύσιν, xxxiii 4 σοβαροῖς ἴχνεσι. The adjective and its cognates are not found in Homer, Hesiod, the early iambic, elegiac, and lyric poets, tragedy, Callimachus, Theocritus, or the Hellenistic epigrammatists. It was below the level of poetry. In comedy and classical prose it is rare, and its meaning, *impetuous*, is different from that which prevails in later authors, *haughty*. It is not found in Thucydides, Plato, Demosthenes, or Aristotle. The only example in Xenophon is *Equ.* 10.17, ἵππον ἐλευθέριον καὶ ἐθελουργὸν καὶ ἱππαστὴν καὶ θυμοειδῆ καὶ σοβαρόν, *impetuous*. Cf. [Demosth.] *Neaer.* 59.37 σοβαρὸν καὶ ὀλίγωρον εἰδυῖα αὐτοῦ τὸν τρόπον, *violent*, as the context shows; Ar. *Nub.* 406 (ἄνεμος) φέρεται σοβαρός, *violent*; *Plut.* 872 ὡς σοβαρὸς εἰσελήλυθεν | ὁ συκοφάντης. δῆλον ὅτι βουλιμιᾶι, *impetuous*; *Pax* 83 σοβαρῶς opposed to ἠρέμα; 944

(αὔρα) σοβαρὰ κατέχει, *rushing*; *Ach.* 673 σοβαρὸν μέλος, a *rousing* tune; Menander *Pk.* 52 ὁ σοβαρὸς ἡμῖν...καὶ πολεμικός, *Kolax* 95 σοβαρὸς μὲν ὁ λόγος, *violent*; Aristophon *fr.* 11.5 θρασὺς καὶ σοβαρός, of Eros, *violent*.

Probably the earliest examples of the word in verse apart from comedy, and in the sense 'haughty', are [Theocritus] 20.15 σοβαρόν μ' ἐγέλαξεν, and [Plato] *A.P.* 6.1.1, σοβαρὸν γελάσασα; it is unlikely that these are earlier than the second century B.C. There is no example of the word in *Hellenistic Epigrams*; in *The Garland of Philip*, only Antiphilus 5.308.4 = *PG* 868, ὦ σοβαρή, addressed to a street-girl, and Geminus *Plan.* 103.3 = *PG* 2374, σοβαρὸν βρίμημα, of Heracles, where the older meaning *violent* reappears, as in anon. *A.P.* 5.82.1 ὦ σοβαρὴ βαλάνισσα.

The word is not found in the satirical epigrams of the first and second centuries A.D., or in Oppian, or in the 2,138 inscriptional epigrams assembled by Peek. Strato has it once, 12.185. 1–2 τοὺς σοβαροὺς τούτους καὶ τοὺς περιπορφυροσήμους παῖδας.

The adverb occurs in Polybius once, in Plutarch often. Lucian has the word very seldom, Longus (1.7) once only, Diogenes Laertius once only (6.24, the verb κατασοβαρεύειν), Alciphron not at all. Aelian *H.A.* 11.4 has σοβαρῶς in the sense 'solemnly'.

In brief, this is a word below the level of poetry and literary prose, rare even in comedy. It makes a few appearances in the late Hellenistic and early Imperial periods, but still very seldom in dignified verse. There is only one period in which it is freely admitted to the higher poetry, and that is the period of the *Cycle* of Agathias. By that time the prejudice against the word has wholly disappeared, and the most elegant writers use it without reserve. Agathias has it in *A.P.* 5.218.1, 273.2, 273.8, 280.8, 294.5, 299.5, 11.382.14; Paulus in 5.217.6; Irenaeus in 5.249.1 and 251.4. In all but one (Agathias 5.218.1) of these places it means *haughty*, as in Rufinus. The fact that Rufinus has no prejudice against the word, but uses it freely, suggests that he is not very far from the period of the *Cycle*. In the fourth century – the latest possible period for Rufinus – Palladas has the adjective once, 5.257.2, of a proud beauty; nor was it then considered below the dignity of the Emperor's prose (Julian 311D, 319D; cf. Priscus p. 311 Dindorf, βαδίζων σοβαρῶς, of Attila = *superbus incessu*, as Jordanes puts it, *Got.* 35.182).

(2) σπάταλος. There seems to be no trace of this word and its cognates earlier than the verb σπαταλάω in Polybius (36.17.7). The verb is extremely rare thereafter: to the unimpressive sources cited by the Lexica (only the Septuagint, Theano, Diogenes, Clem. Alex., *IG* 14.2002 = Peek 1146.7, II–III A.D.; Arndt & Gingrich add three examples from the New Testament and other early Christian writers) may be added Heitsch, *Die gr. Dichter-Fr. d. Röm. Kaiserzeit* LVIII 61 (papyrus *saec.* II A.D.), σπαταλῶσα; κατασπαταλᾶν occurs in the Septuagint and in Lucianus *A.P.* 11.402.2.

The noun σπατάλη, *luxury*, is very rare before the sixth century A.D.: it occurs in the Septuagint, in Nicarchus *A.P.* 11.17.5 and in Lucianus 11.402.1.[1]

The adjective σπάταλος appears first by implication in Petronius 23.3 σπαταλοκίναιδος, and in the name *Spatale* in Martial 2.52; thereafter only (once each) in Soranus, Symmachus, and Eusebius.

It is plain that σπαταλ-, though common in the vernacular (as Petronius and Martial prove), was below the level of literature. Good prose-writers avoid it (there is no example in Lucian), and no verse-writer uses it except the satirical epigrammatists Nicarchus and Lucillius (only once each) and the humble composers of Peek 1146 and Heitsch LVIII.

It must therefore be significant that Rufinus agrees with the *Cycle*-poets in using σπάταλος freely. There is no longer any prejudice against its admission by the most elegant writers. Rufinus has the adjective in v 2, v 6, and IX 6, the noun in IX 4. In the *Cycle*, σπατάλη occurs in Agathias 5.302.2, Damocharis 7.206.6, and Macedonius 5.271.3, σπατάλημα in

---

[1] In the sense *bracelet*, the noun appears in *SIG* 1184.1 (III B.C.) and in Agathias 6.74.8; *spatalium* in Juba *ap.* Plin. *N.H.* 13.142 and a few Roman inscriptions.

Agathias 9.642.1. Thereafter both σοβαρός and σπάταλος remained – as they are in modern Greek – common words.

(3) The conclusion drawn from the admission to elegant poetry of words hitherto excluded from it, σοβαρός and σπάταλος, in Rufinus and the *Cycle* only, would probably be reinforced by other examples if our information were fuller:

(*a*) xviii 2 ἐρωμανίη: this seems to be a very late compound. The adjective ἐρωμανής appears first in Oppian *Hal.* 4.403 (in Diod. Sic. 30.22 the normal prose-form ἐρωτομαν- should be restored, if indeed the text is otherwise correct), the verb ἐρωμανεῖν first in [Oppian] *Cyn.* 3.368; the noun is found only in Rufinus and the *Cycle* (Agathias 5.220.2, Paulus 5.255.12, 256.4, 293.2; the verb in Agathias 5.267.10).[1]

(*b*) xv 1 ἀφελής, *bold, brazen*: it is worth noting that the un-complimentary sense of this adjective, apparent in Rufinus, is common only in the sixth century A.D. and later (*Thesaurus s.v.* 2625–6); its usual meaning in all earlier periods is the opposite, *simple, artless*. This may be another indication that the date of Rufinus should be placed as far forward as possible. It seems odd that the same word might mean either *artful* or *artless*. In its first appearance, Theognis 1211, μή μ' ἀφελῶς παίζουσα φίλους δέννα3ε τοκῆας, the sense is plainly uncomplimentary, but there is no other example of that use before Rufinus except Aristides *or.* 2.116 ἀφελῶς καὶ ἀνειμένως (see Pearson on Soph. *fr.* 723).

(*c*) xxiv 1 μονάσασαν: the evidence indicates that this is a verb which would not have been used by an elegant poet in the earlier centuries A.D. There is indeed no other example of it in verse of any period. It is a word for scholars and eccle-siastics: Herodian (2.913) and Apollonius Dyscolus (*synt.* 191.2) use it of 'unique' phenomena or in the sense *standing alone*, in grammarians' contexts (*cf.* Ap. Dysc. *synt.* 265.19 μονά3ειν ἄνευ συνδέσμου); the churchmen use it to describe monks living in solitude,[2] and that is the sense in Iamblichus

---

[1] See A. W. James, *Studies in the Language of Oppian of Cilicia* (Amsterdam 1970) 96 ff.

[2] *Thesaurus s.v.* 1158–9, Arndt & Gingrich *s.v.* p. 529.

vit. Pythag. 3.14 ἐμόναҙεν, *lived by himself*; *cf.* 35.253 μονάҙειν ἐν ταῖς ἐρημίαις. The use in Rufinus, of one who happens to be unaccompanied, has no parallel except in Psalm 102.7 στρουθίον μονάҙον ἐπὶ δώματι, *a sparrow alone on the house-top.*

(*d*) v 4 σύνοδος: this Aristotelian term for sexual intercourse is altogether avoided by the amatory poets before Rufinus; it may be significant that its only other appearance in verse is in the *Cycle*, Macedonius 5.271.6 (with double meaning).

THEMES AND MOTIFS

Many of Rufinus' themes are familiar, especially from the *Garlands* of Meleager and Philip: II, make merry, for life is brief; III, the kiss that reaches the soul; VI, girls preferred to boys; VII, IX, XXX, XXXVII, the revenge of old age; X, the proud boy humbled; XIII, woman should be neither very thin nor very fat; XV, neither wanton nor prude; XVII, the harlot and the ship; XIX, XXIII, woman ageing but still beautiful; XXVI, XXXV, girls, goddesses, and Graces; XXVIII, bloom and beauty flower and fade; XXXII, XXXVI, love should be mutual; XXXIV, the alliance of Eros and Bacchus invincible; XX, poverty less unendurable than love.

Some, however, have no parallel in the Anthology: IV, the beauty who deserves a Praxiteles; V, slave-girl preferred to luxurious lady; VIII, the poet the willing slave of his mistress; XI, XII, beauty-competitions; XIV, XVI, girls caught in the act and evicted; XVIII, the sleepy lover; XXI, XXVII, girls bathing; XXIV, a prayer for mercy; XXV, a second judgement of Paris; XXIX, a seduction and its consequences; XXXI, a girl reluctant to confess her love. Some of these, but by no means all of them, may be classed as unusual variations on familiar themes; on the credit side may be added the originality of the epistle-form of I and the *kondax*-motif of XXII.

In general, the themes and motifs of Rufinus are much more like those of the two *Garlands* than of any later period; and not many of the *Garlands'* authors show greater originality in choice and treatment of subject.

NAMES OF WOMEN

Thirteen[1] different women's names appear in the thirty-seven epigrams. Most of them are either unique or rare, but they do not suggest a setting in any particular period.

Amymona seems to be unique except for the one example in myth. *Boöpis* (if a real name) is unique. *Elpis* is common in the early Christian period. *Europa* is very rare except in myth, but occurs in Antipater of Thessalonica 5.109 = *PG* liii. *Maeonis* is unique. *Melissa* is quite common, *Melissias* unique. *Melita* is attested from Leonidas to Agathias. *Philippa* does not reappear in the Anthology but was common in life (Kirchner 14344–8). *Prodica* seems to be unique. *Rhodocleia* is very rare (Leontius *Plan.* 283). *Rhodopa* is attested from Antipater of Sidon to Irenaeus. *Thalia* is very rare (Kirchner 6567, I A.D., Agathias 7.568).

THE DATE OF RUFINUS:
GENERAL CONCLUSION

The relation between Rufinus and Ausonius is good evidence for the conclusion that Rufinus lived not later than the fourth century A.D. The lower limit remains doubtful. The evidence of vocabulary is against the period 50–150 and indicates rather a later than an earlier time within the period 150–400. The same conclusion is suggested (but only suggested) by the frequency of gross errors in scansion, ἐκδέδυκας, ἐρῖσασα, ἠρασάμην, and probably κέκραγεν. A preference for the latest possible period, the fourth century, seems reasonable.

---

[1] Not counting the made-up names *Kerkourion* and *Lembion*.

THE EPIGRAMS

SIGLA

P = codex Anthologiae Palatinae (Palat. 23 + Paris. Suppl. gr. 384)

J = codicis P partim librarius, alibi lemmatista

C = codicis P corrector

Pl = codex Anthologiae Planudeae (Ven. Marc. 481) ab ipso Max. Planude scriptus: Pl^a = codicis foll. 2–76 (abest Rufinus a Pl^b = codicis foll. 81^v–100)

App. B.-V. = Appendix Barberino-Vaticana (cod. V = Vaticanus gr. n. 240, saec. xvi; cod. M = Barberinus gr. 1.123, saec. xiv et xvi), ed. L. Sternbach (Lips. 1890)

ac = ante correctionem

aC = ante correctionem a C factam

pc = post correctionem

s.a.n. = sine auctoris nomine

apogr. = apographa codicum PPl a viris doctis facta; vid. Gow & Page *The Greek Anthology: Hellenistic Epigrams* i. xliii–xlv

In the note beginning the apparatus for each epigram, square brackets enclose the source of what immediately follows; thus in xxvi the note 'A.P. 5.73 (caret Pl) [J ad v. 6] 'Ρουφίνου [C] καὶ τοῦτο δὲ τὸ ἐπίγραμμα 'Ρουφίνου [J] εἰς 'Ροδόκλειάν τινα κτλ.' means that the lemmatist 'J' wrote the name 'Ρουφίνου and the *lemma* εἰς 'Ροδόκλειάν τινα κτλ., and the Corrector 'C' wrote καὶ τοῦτο δὲ κτλ. In viii, the heading 'A.P. 5.22, Pl^a [PPl] τοῦ αὐτοῦ' means that P and Pl have τοῦ αὐτοῦ.

I

'Ρουφῖνος τῆι 'μῆι γλυκερωτάτηι 'Ελπίδι πολλά
χαίρειν, εἰ χαίρειν χωρὶς ἐμοῦ δύνασαι.
οὐκέτι βαστάζω, μὰ τὰ σ' ὄμματα, τὴν φιλέρημον
καὶ τὴν μουνολεχῆ σεῖο διαζυγίην,
ἀλλ' αἰεὶ δακρύοισι πεφυρμένος ἢ 'πὶ Κορησσόν   5
ἔρχομαι ἢ μεγάλης νηὸν ἐς 'Αρτέμιδος.
αὔριον ἀλλὰ πάτρη με δεδέξεται, ἐς δὲ σὸν ὄμμα
πτήσομαι· ἐρρῶσθαι μυρία σ' εὐχόμενος.

II

λουσάμενοι, Προδίκη, πυκασώμεθα, καὶ τὸν ἄκρατον
ἕλκωμεν κύλικας μείζονας αἰρόμενοι.
βαιὸς ὁ χαιρόντων ἐστὶν βίος· εἶτα τὰ λοιπά
γῆρας κωλύσει καὶ τὸ τέλος θάνατος.

III

Εὐρώπης τὸ φίλαμα καὶ ἢν ἄχρι χείλεος ἔλθηι
ἡδύ γε, κἂν ψαύσηι μοῦνον ἄχρι στόματος·

I A.P. 5.9 'Ρουφίνου, Pl^a in duo discerptum, vv. 1–2 τοῦ αὐτοῦ (sc. 'Ρουφίνου), 3–8 ἄδηλον
[J] εἰς 'Ελπίδα εἴτε ἑταίραν τινὰ εἴτε τὴν οὕτω καλουμένην· ἐρωτικόν
1 γλυκερωτάτη P   2 δύνασαι Pl: δύναται P   post δύναται in P erasa
est clausula; peculiare igitur epigramma erat primum distichon in P^ac
sicut in Pl   4 μουνολοχὴ P^ac   5 ἢ 'πὶ Κορησσόν Hecker: ἢ ἐπιορκήσων
PPl   7 πατρι P^ac   8 μυρία σ' Plan. edd. vett.: μυρίας PPl, μυρίος C

II A.P. 5.12 'Ρουφίνου, Pl^a τοῦ αὐτοῦ (sc. 'Ρουφίνου); Sud. s.v. πυκάζει
[J] εἰς Προδίκην ἑταίραν
1 Προδόκη P^ac Sud.   2 ἀράμενοι Pl

III A.P. 5.14 'Ρουφίνου, Pl^a τοῦ αὐτοῦ (sc. 'Ρουφίνου)
[J] εἰς Εὐρώπην τὴν ἑταίραν
1 φίλημα Pl   2 ἡδύ γε P: ἥδει Pl   ψαύη Pl

ψαύει δ' οὐκ ἄκροις τοῖς χείλεσιν, ἀλλ' ἐρίσασα
τὸ στόμα τὴν ψυχὴν ἐξ ὀνύχων ἀνάγει.

IV

ποῦ νῦν Πραξιτέλης, ποῦ δ' αἱ χέρες αἱ Πολυκλείτου
αἱ ταῖς πρόσθε τέχναις πνεῦμα χαριζόμεναι;
τίς πλοκάμους Μελίτης εὐώδεας ἢ πυρόεντα
ὄμματα καὶ δειρῆς φέγγος ἀποπλάσεται;
ποῦ πλάσται, ποῦ δ' εἰσὶ λιθοξόοι; ἔπρεπε τοίηι
μορφῆι νηὸν ἔχειν ὡς μακάρων ξοάνωι.

V

μᾶλλον τῶν σοβαρῶν τὰς δουλίδας ἐκλεγόμεσθα,
οἱ μὴ τοῖς σπατάλοις κλέμμασι τερπόμενοι.
ταῖς μὲν χρὼς ἀπόδωδε μύρου, σοβαρόν τε φρύαγμα,
καὶ μέχρι κινδύνου† ἑσπομένη σύνοδος·
ταῖς δὲ χάρις καὶ χρὼς ἴδιος καὶ λέκτρον ἕτοιμον
†δώροις ἐκ σπατάλοις† οὐκ ἀλεγιζόμενον.
μιμοῦμαι Πύρρον τὸν Ἀχιλλέος, ὃς προέκρινεν
Ἑρμιόνης ἀλόχου τὴν λάτριν Ἀνδρομάχην.

3 ἐρείσασα Pl (ἐρείσ- in ἐρίσ- mutat, mox ἐρύσασα coni.)

IV A.P. 5.15, Pl^a [PPl] τοῦ αὐτοῦ (sc. ῾Ρουφίνου)
[J] εἰς Μελίτην ἑταίραν
2 αἱ ταῖς Pl: αὐταῖς P   3 τί P^{ac}   5 τοίη C: τῆ** P, τῆιδε Pl   6
ξοάνωι Salmasius: -νων P, -νον Pl

V A.P. 5.18 (caret Pl), App. B.-V. 48 [P App.] ῾Ρουφίνου
[J] ἐρωτικόν, προκρῖνον τὰς δούλας τῶν ἐλευθέρων [C] ἔστι δὲ ἡ τοῦ γράμ-
ματος ἔννοια ὡς ἄριστα ἔχουσα
1 ἐκλεγώμεσθα P^{ac}, -γόμεθα App.   2 σπατάλοις C: ἀπαταλοῖς P, σπατάλων App.   3 ταῖς P: τοῖς App. cod. M, τῆς cod. V   5 τῆς App. cod.
M   accent. ἑτοῖμον P   6 om. App.

54

VI

οὐκέτι παιδομανὴς ὡς πρίν ποτε, νῦν δὲ καλοῦμαι
θηλυμανής, καὶ νῦν δίσκος ἐμοὶ κρόταλον.
ἀντὶ δέ μοι παίδων ἀδόλου χροὸς ἤρεσε γύψου
χρώματα καὶ φύκους ἄνθος ἐπεισόδιον.
βοσκήσει δελφῖνας ὁ δενδροκόμης Ἐρύμανθος   5
καὶ πολιὸν πόντου κῦμα θοὰς ἐλάφους.

VII

οὐκ ἔλεγον, Προδίκη, γηράσκομεν; οὐ προεφώνουν
"ἥξουσιν ταχέως αἱ διαλυσίφιλοι";
νῦν ῥυτίδες καὶ θρὶξ πολιὴ καὶ σῶμα ῥακῶδες
καὶ στόμα τὰς προτέρας οὐκέτ' ἔχον χάριτας.
μή τίς σοι, μετέωρε, προσέρχεται ἢ κολακεύων   5
λίσσεται; ὡς δὲ τάφον νῦν σε παρερχόμεθα.

VIII

σοί με λάτριν γλυκύδωρος Ἔρως παρέδωκε, Βοῶπι,
ταῦρον ὑποζεύξας εἰς πόθον αὐτόμολον,
αὐτοθελῆ, πάνδουλον, ἑκούσιον, αὐτοκέλευστον,
αἰτήσοντα πικρὴν μήποτ' ἐλευθερίην
ἄχρι φίλης πολιῆς καὶ γήραος. ὄμμα βάλοι δέ   5
μήποτ' ἐφ' ἡμετέραις ἐλπίσι βασκανίη.

VI A.P. 5.19, Pl[a] [PPl] τοῦ αὐτοῦ (sc. ᾽Ρουφίνου); Sud. s.vv. κρόταλος,
δισκεύων (1 καὶ νῦν καλοῦμαι – 2), ἐπεισόδιον (3 ἤρεσε – 4)
[J] ἐρωτικὸν ἀλλόκοτον.
4 χρίσματα Pl

VII A.P. 5.21 ᾽Ρουφίνου, Pl[a] τοῦ αὐτοῦ (sc. ᾽Ρουφίνου)
[J] εἰς Προδίκην ἑταίραν
1 Προδόκη P[ac]   5 κολακευτῶν P

VIII A.P. 5.22, Pl[a] [PPl] τοῦ αὐτοῦ (sc. ᾽Ρουφίνου); Sud. s.v. Παλαμήδης
(5 ὄμμα – 6)
[J] εἰς Βοῶπιν τὴν ἑταίραν
2 ταῦρον Brunck: γαῦρον PPl

55   5-2

IX

ποῦ σοι κεῖνα, Μέλισσα, τὰ χρύσεα καὶ περίοπτα
τῆς πολυθρυλήτου κάλλεα φαντασίης;
ποῦ δ' ὀφρύες καὶ γαῦρα φρονήματα καὶ μέγας αὐχήν
καὶ σοβαρῶν ταρσῶν χρυσοφόρος σπατάλη;
5 νῦν πενιχρὴ ψαφαρή τε κόμην, περὶ ποσσὶ παχεῖα·
ταῦτα τὰ τῶν σπατάλων τέρματα παλλακίδων.

X

νῦν μοι "χαῖρε" λέγεις, ὅτε σου τὸ πρόσωπον ἀπῆλθεν
κεῖνο τὸ τῆς λύγδου, βάσκανε, λαότερον·
νῦν μοι προσπαίζεις, ὅτε τὰς τρίχας ἠφάνικάς σου
τὰς ἐπὶ τοῖς σοβαροῖς αὐχέσι πλαζομένας.
5 μηκέτι μοι, μετέωρε, προσέρχεο μηδὲ συνάντα·
ἀντὶ ῥόδου γὰρ ἐγὼ τὴν βάτον οὐ δέχομαι.

XI

πυγὰς αὐτὸς ἔκρινα τριῶν, εἵλοντο γὰρ αὐταί
δείξασαι γυμνῶν ἀστεροπὴν μελέων.
καί ῥ' ἡ μὲν τροχαλοῖς σφραγιζομένη γελασίνοις
λευκῆι ἀπὸ γλουτῶν ἤνθεεν εὐαφίηι,

IX A.P. 5.27 Ῥουφίνου, Pl^a ἄδηλον
[J] εἰς Μέλισσαν τὴν ἑταίραν
2 -θρυλλήτου PPl 5 κόμην περὶ Jacobs: κόμη παρὰ P, κόμη τ' ἐπὶ Pl
παχεῖα Meineke: τραχεῖα P, βραχεῖα Pl

X A.P. 5.28 τοῦ αὐτοῦ (sc. Ῥουφίνου), Pl^a ἄδηλον
[J] εἰς πόρνην γηράσασαν καὶ τοῖς ἐρασταῖς ὑποβαίνουσαν [C] εἰς μειράκιον
4 πλαζομένας; C

XI A.P. 5.35 Ῥουφίνου, Pl^a (vv. 9–10 tantum) τοῦ αὐτοῦ (sc. Ῥουφίνου),
App. B.-V. 13 Ῥουφίνου cod. M, Διονύσου cod. V; Sud. s.v. γελασίνοις
(3–4)
[J] εἰς πόρνας, ἀναίσχυντον καὶ σαπρὸν καὶ ὅλον γέμον ἀναίδειαν
1 αὗται P App. 2 γυμνῶν Toup: γυμνὴν P App. 3 σφραγιζομένη P:
φθεγγομένη (M) et σφιγγομένη (V) App. 4 λευκῆι... εὐαφίηι App. cod.

τῆς δὲ διαιρομένης φοινίσσετο χιονέη σάρξ   5
πορφυρέοιο ῥόδου μᾶλλον ἐρυθροτέρη,
ἡ δὲ γαληνιόωσα χαράσσετο κύματι κωφῶι
αὐτομάτη τρυφερῶι χρωτὶ σαλευομένη.
εἰ ταύτας ὁ κριτὴς ὁ θεῶν ἐθεήσατο πυγάς,
οὐκέτ᾿ ἂν οὐδ᾿ ἐσιδεῖν ἤθελε τὰς προτέρας.   10

XII

ἤρισαν ἀλλήλαις Ῥοδόπη Μελίτη Ῥοδόκλεια,
τῶν τρισσῶν τίς ἔχει κρείσσονα μηριόνην,
καί με κριτὴν εἵλοντο· καὶ ὡς θεαὶ αἱ περίβλεπτοι
ἔστησαν γυμναί, νέκταρι λειβόμεναι.
καὶ Ῥοδόπης μὲν ἔλαμπε μέσος μηρῶν πολύτιμος   5
⟨   ⟩   5α
⟨   ⟩   5β
οἶα ῥοδὼν †πολιῶι† σχιζόμενος ζεφύρωι·
τῆς δὲ Ῥοδοκλείης ὑάλωι ἴσος, ὑγρομέτωπος,
οἶα καὶ ἐν νηῶι πρωτογλυφὲς ξόανον.
ἀλλὰ σαφῶς ἃ πέπονθε Πάρις διὰ τὴν κρίσιν εἰδώς
τὰς τρεῖς ἀθανάτας εὐθὺ συνεστεφάνουν.   10

V: λευκὴ ... εὐαφίην P Sud., λευκὴν ... εὐαφίην C primo, postea λευκή ...
εὐαφίη idem, λευκῆι ... εὐαφίη App. cod. M   9 ἐθεάσατο κούρας Pl

XII A.P. 5.36, Plᵃ [PPl] τοῦ αὐτοῦ (sc. Ῥουφίνου)
[J] ὅμοιον, ἀναίσχυντον καὶ σαπρότατον
2 ἔχει κάλλος ἀρειότερον Pl   4 γυμναί P: μούνωι Plᵃᶜ, ῥοδάνωι vel ῥοδίνωι
Plᵖᶜ   λειβόμεναι Jacobs: λειπόμεναι PPl   5–8 om. Pl   5α–5β: versus
duos de Melita intercidisse vidit Jacobs; lacunam post 5 statuit Page, post 6
vel 8 edd. priores   6 ῥόδων P   8 post h.v. distichon 5–6 ex Rufini epigr.
xxi τὸν δ᾿ ὑπεροιδαίνοντα ... ἠδύνατο repetit P, del. Jacobs   10 ἀθανά-
τους Pl   εὐθὺς PᵃᶜPlᵃᶜ

XIII

μήτ' ἰσχνὴν λίην περιλάμβανε μήτε παχεῖαν,
τούτων δ' ἀμφοτέρων τὴν μεσότητα θέλε.
τῆι μὲν γὰρ λείπει σαρκῶν χύσις, ἡ δὲ περισσήν
κέκτηται· λεῖπον μὴ θέλε μηδὲ πλέον.

XIV

τίς γυμνὴν οὕτω σε καὶ ἐξέβαλεν καὶ ἔδειρεν;
τίς ψυχὴν λιθίνην εἶχε καὶ οὐκ ἔβλεπεν;
μοιχὸν ἴσως ηὕρηκεν ἀκαίρως κεῖνος ἐσελθών·
γινόμενον· πᾶσαι τοῦτο ποοῦσι, τέκνον.
5   πλὴν ἀπὸ νῦν, ὅταν ἐστὶν ἔσω, κεῖνος δ' ὅταν ἔξω,
τὸ πρόθυρον σφήνου, μὴ πάλι ταὐτὸ πάθηις.

XV

μισῶ τὴν ἀφελῆ, μισῶ τὴν σώφρονα λίαν·
ἡ μὲν γὰρ βραδέως, ἡ δὲ θέλει ταχέως.

XIII A.P. 5.37 (caret Pl) τοῦ αὐτοῦ (sc. ῾Ρουφίνου), App. B.-V. 19 ῾Ρουφίνου
[J] ὁμοίως
1 παχείην App.   3 σαρκὸς App. cod. M

XIV A.P. 5.41 ῾Ρουφίνου, Plᵃ, App. B.-V. 15 [Pl App.] τοῦ αὐτοῦ (sc.
῾Ρουφίνου)
[J] πρός τινα πόρνην· χλευαστικόν
epigr. om. App. cod. M, 3–6 om. cod. V   1 ἔδηρεν Plˢˢᶜʳ   2 καὶ ου κέ
βλέπε P   3 ηὕρ- P: εὕρ- Pl   post ἐσελθὼν signum interrogationis scr.
Pl   4 γιγνόμενον Pl   ποιοῦσι Pl

XV A.P. 5.42 τοῦ αὐτοῦ (sc. ῾Ρουφίνου), Plᵃ s.a.n.; schol. Ald. ad Ar.
Equ. 524; Sud. s.vv. ἀφέλεια, μισῶ (1)
[J] εἰς πόρνας
1 λίην schol.

XVI

ἐκβάλλει γυμνήν τις, ἐπὰν εὕρηι ποτὲ μοιχόν,
ὡς μὴ μοιχεύσας, ὡς ἀπὸ Πυθαγόρου·
εἶτα, τέκνον, κλαίουσα καταδρύψεις τὸ πρόσωπον
καὶ παραριγώσεις μαινομένου προθύροις;
ἔκμαξαι, μὴ κλαῖε, τέκνον, χεὑρήσομεν ἄλλον,   5
τὸν μὴ καὶ τὸ βλέπειν εἰδότα καὶ τὸ δέρειν.

XVII

Λέμβιον, ἡ δ' ἑτέρα Κερκούριον, αἱ δύ' ἑταῖραι,
αἰὲν ἐφορμοῦσιν τῶι Σαμίων λιμένι.
ἀλλά, νέοι, πανδημὶ τὰ ληιστρικὰ τῆς Ἀφροδίτης
φεύγεθ'· ὁ συμμίξας καὶ καταδὺς πίεται.

XVIII

πολλάκις ἠρασάμην σε λαβὼν ἐν νυκτί, Θάλεια,
πληρῶσαι θαλερῆι θυμὸν ἐρωμανίηι·
νῦν δ' ὅτε ⟨μοι⟩ γυμνὴ γλυκεροῖς μελέεσσι πέπλησαι,
ἔκλυτος ὑπναλέωι γυῖα κέκμηκα κόπωι.
θυμὲ τάλαν, τί πέπονθας; ἀνέγρεο μηδ' ἀπόκαμνε·   5
ζητήσεις ταύτην τὴν ὑπερευτυχίην.

XVI A.P. 5.43, Plᵃ [PPl] τοῦ αὐτοῦ (sc. ῾Ρουφίνου)
[J] ὁμοίως
1 τις C Pl: τίς P   ἐπὴν Pl   3 καταδρύψεις Pl: κατατρίψεις P   6 τὸν
μὴ καὶ τὸ Jacobs: τὸν μηκέτι P, μηκέτι τὸν Pl

XVII A.P. 5.44 (caret Pl) τοῦ αὐτοῦ (sc. ῾Ρουφίνου)
[J] εἰς τὰς ἑταίρας Λέμβιον καὶ Κερκούριον. εἰσὶ δὲ ταῦτα τὰ ὀνόματα
μικρῶν καραβίων τῶν παρ' ἡμῖν σανδάλων

XVIII A.P. 5.47 (caret Pl) ῾Ρουφίνου; An. Par. Cramer 4.287.15
[J] εἰς Θάλειαν τὴν ἑαυτοῦ ἑταίραν
3 μοι suppl. apogr.   5 τάλαν C: τάλας P An. Par.

XIX

ὄμματα μὲν χρύσεια καὶ ὑαλόεσσα παρειή
καὶ στόμα πορφυρέης τερπνότερον κάλυκος,
δειρὴ λυγδινέη καὶ στήθεα μαρμαίροντα
καὶ πόδες ἀργυρέης λευκότεροι Θέτιδος·
5   εἰ δέ τι καὶ πλοκαμῖσι διαστίλβουσιν ἄκανθαι,
τῆς λευκῆς καλάμης οὐδὲν ἐπιστρέφομαι.

XX

καὶ πενίη καὶ ἔρως δύο μοι κακά· καὶ τὸ μὲν οἴσω
κούφως, πῦρ δὲ φέρειν Κύπριδος οὐ δύναμαι.

XXI

παρθένος ἀργυρόπεζος ἐλούετο, χρύσεα μαζῶν
χρωτὶ γαλακτοπαγεῖ μῆλα διαινομένη·
πυγαὶ δ' ἀλλήλαις περιηγέες εἰλίσσοντο
ὕδατος ὑγροτέρωι χρωτὶ σαλευόμεναι·
5   τὸν δ' ὑπεροιδαίνοντα κατέσκεπε πεπταμένη χείρ
οὐχ ὅλον Εὐρώταν ἀλλ' ὅσον ἠδύνατο.

XIX A.P. 5.48 τοῦ αὐτοῦ (sc. Ῥουφίνου), Pl[a] s.a.n.
[J] εἰς κόρην· ἔπαινος τοῦ κάλλους αὐτῆς
1 χρύσεα P[ac]   ὑελόεσσα ?P[ac]   5 ἀκάνθας P   6 οὐδὲ P[ac]   ἐπιστρεφόμην ?P[ac]

XX A.P. 5.50 (caret Pl) ἀδέσποτον, App. B.-V. 49 Ῥουφίνου
1 μοι om. P[ac]

XXI A.P. 5.60 (caret Pl) Ῥουφίνου, App. B.-V. bis, 14 et post 49 (1–4)
τοῦ αὐτοῦ (sc. Ῥουφίνου); Sud. s.v. Εὐρώτας (5–6); Eust. Od. 1478.39 (6)
[J] εἰς παρθένον λουομένην
1 ἀργυρόπεζα et μαζόν utroque loco App.   2 γαλακτοπαγῇ App. 14
3 πηγαὶ P[ac] App. 14 cod. M   πυριηγέες ἐλίσσοντο P[ac]   5–6 om.
App. utroque loco; vid. etiam xii 8 n.   6 ἐδύνατο P[ac]

XXII

τῆι κυανοβλεφάρωι παίзων κόνδακα Φιλίππηι
ἐξ αὐτῆς κραδίης ἡδὺ γελᾶν ἐπόουν·
"δώδεκά σοι βέβληκα, καὶ αὔριον ἄλλα βαλῶ σοι
ἢ πλέον ἠὲ πάλιν δώδεκ' ἐπιστάμενος."
εἶπα, κελευομένη ⟨δ'⟩ ἦλθεν· γελάσας δὲ πρὸς αὐτήν
"εἴθε σε καὶ νύκτωρ ἐγρομένην ἐκάλουν."

XXIII

οὔ πώ σοι τὸ καλὸν χρόνος ἔσβεσεν, ἀλλ' ἔτι πολλά
λείψανα τῆς προτέρης σώιзεται ἡλικίης,
καὶ Χάριτες μίμνουσιν ἀγήραοι, οὐδὲ τὸ καλόν
τῶν ἱλαρῶν μήλων ἢ ῥόδον ἐξέφυγεν.
ὦ πόσσους κατέφλεξε τὸ πρὶν θεοείκελον †κάλλος† 5
⟨   ⟩

XXIV

εὐκαίρως μονάσασαν ἰδὼν Προδίκην ἱκέτευον,
καὶ τῶν ἀμβροσίων ἁψάμενος γονάτων
"σῶσον" ἔφην "ἄνθρωπον ἀπολλύμενον παρὰ μικρόν,
καὶ φεῦγον зωῆς πνεῦμα σύ μοι χάρισαι."

XXII A.P. 5.61 (caret Pl) τοῦ αὐτοῦ (sc. 'Ρουφίνου)
[J] εἰς Φιλίππην τὴν ἑταίραν
5 εἶπα...δ' ἦλθεν Ludwich: εἶτα...ἦλθεν P   6 ἐγρομένην Stadtmüller:
ἐρχομένην P

XXIII A.P. 5.62 (caret Pl) τοῦ αὐτοῦ (sc. 'Ρουφίνου)
[J] εἰς ἀνώνυμόν τινα γυναῖκα
1 χρόνος Salmasius: ὁ χρόνος P   6 versum om. spatio vac. relicto P;
marg. inf. scr. C зτ ὁππότε πρωτόπλουν (hoc C²: τὴν πρώτην ?C¹) ἔτρεχες
ἡλικίην. ἄλλως· ἡνίκα πρωτοβόλων λάμψεν ἀπὸ βλεφάρων

XXIV A.P. 5.66 ἀδέσποτον [C] 'Ρουφίνου, Plᵃ τοῦ αὐτοῦ (sc. 'Ρουφίνου)
[J] εἰς Προδίκην ἐρωμένην

5   ταῦτα λέγοντος ἔκλαυσεν, ἀποψήσασα δὲ δάκρυ
ταῖς τρυφεραῖς ἡμᾶς χερσὶν ὑπεξέλαβεν.

XXV

αλλὰς ἐσαθρήσασα καὶ "Ηρη χρυσοπέδιλος
Μαιονίδ᾽ ἐκ κραδίης ἴαχον ἀμφότεραι
"οὐκέτι γυμνούμεσθα· κρίσις μία ποιμένος ἀρκεῖ·
οὐ καλὸν ἡττᾶσθαι δὶς περὶ καλλοσύνης."

XXVI

κάλλος ἔχεις Κύπριδος, Πειθοῦς στόμα, σῶμα καὶ ἀκμήν
εἰαρινῶν Ὡρῶν, φθέγμα δὲ Καλλιόπης,
νοῦν καὶ σωφροσύνην Θέμιδος καὶ χεῖρας Ἀθήνης·
σὺν σοὶ δ᾽ αἱ Χάριτες τέσσαρές εἰσι, φίλη.

XXVII

δαίμονες, οὐκ ᾔδειν ὅτι λούεται ⟨ἡ⟩ Κυθέρεια
χερσὶ καταυχενίους λυσαμένη πλοκάμους.
ἱλήκοις, δέσποινα, καὶ ὄμμασιν ἡμετέροισι

6 χερσὶν ἡμᾶς Pl   ὑπεξέλαβεν Hecker: -ἐβαλεν PPl

XXV A.P. 5.69, Plᵃ [PPl] ʻΡουφίνου
[J] εἰς Μαιονίδα κόρην
2 Μαιονὶν Pl   3 γυμνούμεσθα Plan. edd. vett.: -μεθα PPl

XXVI A.P. 5.70, Plᵃ [PPl] τοῦ αὐτοῦ (sc. ʻΡουφίνου)
[J] εἰς ἑταίραν εὔμορφον
2 εἰαριανῶν P   4 αἱ CPl: ἀν vel αὖ P   φίλη Stephanus: φίλαι PPl
(potius Plᵖᶜ opinor; fort. φίλη Plᵃᶜ)

XXVII A.P. 5.73 (caret Pl) [J ad v. 6] ʻΡουφίνου [C] καὶ τοῦτο δὲ τὸ
ἐπίγραμμα ʻΡουφίνου
[J] εἰς ʻΡοδόκλειάν τινα ἑταίραν ὡραίαν
1 ἡ suppl. apogr., om. P

62

μήποτε μηνίσῃς θεῖον ἰδοῦσι τύπον.
νῦν ἔγνων· 'Ροδόκλεια, καὶ οὐ Κύπρις· εἶτα τὸ κάλλος   5
τοῦτο πόθεν; σύ, δοκῶ, τὴν θεὸν ἐκδέδυκας.

XXVIII

πέμπω σοι, 'Ροδόκλεια, τόδε στέφος, ἄνθεσι καλοῖς
αὐτὸς ὑφ' ἡμετέραις πλεξάμενος παλάμαις.
ἔστι κρίνον ῥοδέη τε κάλυξ νοτερή τ' ἀνεμώνη
καὶ νάρκισσος ὑγρὸς καὶ κυαναυγὲς ἴον.
ταῦτα στεψαμένη λῆξον μεγάλαυχος ἐοῦσα·   5
ἀνθεῖς καὶ λήγεις καὶ σὺ καὶ ὁ στέφανος.

XXIX

γείτονα παρθένον εἶχον 'Αμυμώνην, 'Αφροδίτη,
ἥ μου τὴν ψυχὴν ἔφλεγεν οὐκ ὀλίγον.
αὐτή μοι προσέπαιζε, καὶ εἴ ποτε καιρὸς ἐτόλμων·
ἠρυθρία· τί πλέον; τὸν πόνον ᾐσθάνετο.
ἤνυσα πολλὰ καμών. παρακήκοα νῦν ὅτι τίκτει.   5
ὥστε τί ποιοῦμεν; φεύγομεν ἢ μένομεν;

4 μηνίσῃς Salmasius: μνήσῃς P, μνήσῃς C   ἰδοῦσι Salmasius: ἰδοῦσα P

XXVIII A.P. 5.74, Pl^a [PPl] τοῦ αὐτοῦ (sc. 'Ρουφίνου)
[J] εἰς τὴν αὐτὴν 'Ροδόκλειαν
1 καλοῖς P: πλέξας Pl   2 ὑμετέραις ?P^ac   πλεξάμενος P: δρεψάμενος Pl

XXIX A.P. 5.75 τοῦ αὐτοῦ [J] 'Ρουφίνου, Pl^a τοῦ αὐτοῦ (sc. 'Ρουφίνου)
[J] εἴς τινα παρθένον φθαρεῖσαν ὑπ' αὐτοῦ
1 'Αφροδίτη Scaliger: -την PPl   2 ἔφλεξεν P   3 αὐτή Bothe: αὕτη PPl
προσέπαιξε P   ἐτόλμα Pl   4 ἠρυθρίαι C   τὸν πόνον CPl^pc: τῶν
πόνων P, τῶν πόνον Pl^ac

63

RVFINI

XXX

αὕτη πρόσθεν ἔην ἐρατόχροος εἰαρόμασθος
εὔσφυρος εὐμήκης εὔοφρυς εὐπλόκαμος·
ἠλλάχθη δὲ χρόνωι καὶ γήραϊ καὶ πολιαῖσι,
καὶ νῦν τῶν προτέρων οὐδ' ὄναρ οὐδὲν ἔχει,
5   ἀλλοτρίας δὲ τρίχας καὶ ῥυσῶδες ⟨τὸ⟩ πρόσωπον,
οἷον γηράσας οὐδὲ πίθηκος, ἔχει.

XXXI

ἀρνεῖται τὸν ἔρωτα Μελισσιάς, ἀλλὰ τὸ σῶμα
κέκραγεν ὡς βελέων δεξάμενον φαρέτρην·
καὶ βάσις ἀστατέουσα, καὶ ἄστατος ἄσθματος ὁρμή,
καὶ κοῖλαι βλεφάρων ἰοτυπεῖς βάσιες.
5   ἀλλά, Πόθοι, πρὸς μητρὸς ἐυστεφάνου Κυθερείης,
φλέξατε τὴν ἀπιθῆ μέχρις ἐρεῖ "φλέγομαι."

XXXII

εἰ δυσὶν οὐκ ἴσχυσας ἴσην φλόγα, πυρφόρε, καῦσαι,
τὴν ἑνὶ καιομένην ἢ σβέσον ἢ μετάθες.

XXX A.P. 5.76, Pl^a [PPl] τοῦ αὐτοῦ (sc. Ῥουφίνου)
[J] εἰς πόρνην γηράσασαν· σκωπτικόν
3 πολιῆισι Pl   5–6 om. Pl   5 ῥυσῶδες Jacobs: ρυτῶ δὲς P   τὸ
suppl. man. rec. in P

XXXI A.P. 5.87 Ῥουφίνου, Pl^a τοῦ αὐτοῦ (sc. Ῥουφίνου)
[J] εἰς Μελισσιάδα τὴν ἑταίραν
1 Μελησιάς P

XXXII A.P. 5.88, Pl^a [PPl] τοῦ αὐτοῦ (sc. Ῥουφίνου)
2 σβέσον P: σάου Pl

XXXIII

ὑψοῦται Ῥοδόπη τῶι κάλλεϊ, κἤν ποτε "χαῖρε"
εἴπω, ταῖς σοβαραῖς ὀφρύσιν ἠσπάσατο ·
ἤν ποτε καὶ στεφάνους προθύρων ὕπερ ἐκκρεμάσωμαι,
ὀργισθεῖσα πατεῖ τοῖς σοβαροῖς ἴχνεσι.
ὦ ῥυτίδες καὶ γῆρας ἀνηλεές, ἔλθετε θᾶσσον,   5
σπεύσατε · κἂν ὑμεῖς πείσατε τὴν Ῥοδόπην.

XXXIV

ὥπλισμαι πρὸς Ἔρωτα περὶ στέρνοισι λογισμόν,
οὐδέ με νικήσει μοῦνος ἐὼν πρὸς ἕνα.
θνατὸς δ' ἀθανάτωι συστήσομαι. ἢν δὲ βοηθόν
Βάκχον ἔχηι, τί μόνος πρὸς δύ' ἐγὼ δύναμαι;

XXXV

ὄμματ' ἔχεις Ἥρης, Μελίτη, τὰς χεῖρας Ἀθήνης,
τοὺς μαζοὺς Παφίης, τὰ σφυρὰ τῆς Θέτιδος.
εὐδαίμων ὁ βλέπων σε, τρισόλβιος ὅστις ἀκούει,
ἡμίθεος δ' ὁ φιλῶν, ἀθάνατος δ' ὁ γαμῶν.

XXXIII A.P. 5.92 Ῥουφίνου, Pl^a τοῦ αὐτοῦ (sc. Ῥουφίνου)
[J] εἰς Ῥοδόπην τὴν ἑταίραν

XXXIV A.P. 5.93, Pl^a [PPl] τοῦ αὐτοῦ (sc. Ῥουφίνου)
[J] πρὸς Ἔρωτα
2 μοῦνον ἐὼν Pl^ac   3 συνελεύσομαι Pl

XXXV A.P. 5.94, Pl^a [PPl] τοῦ αὐτοῦ (sc. Ῥουφίνου)
[J] εἰς Μελίτην · ὡραῖον
1 Ἀθηνᾶς ?P^ac   4 ἤιθεος P   γαμῶν P: συνών Pl

XXXVI

εἰ μὲν ἐπ' ἀμφοτέροισιν, Ἔρως, ἴσα τόξα τιταίνεις,
εἰ θεός· εἰ δὲ ῥέπεις πρὸς μέρος, οὐ θεὸς εἶ.

XXXVII

μέχρι τίνος, Προδίκη, παρακλαύσομαι; ἄχρι τίνος σε
γουνάσομαι, στερεή, μηδὲν ἀκουόμενος;
ἤδη καὶ λευκαί σοι ἐπισκιρτῶσιν ἔθειραι,
καὶ τάχα μοι δώσεις ὡς Ἑκάβη Πριάμωι.

[XXXVIII]

οὕτως ὑπνώσαις, Κωνώπιον, ὡς ἐμὲ ποιεῖς
κοιμᾶσθαι ψυχροῖς τοῖσδε παρὰ προθύροις·
οὕτως ὑπνώσαις, ἀδικωτάτη, ὡς τὸν ἐραστήν
κοιμίζεις, ἐλέου δ' οὐδ' ὄναρ ἠντίασας.
5   γείτονες οἰκτείρουσι, σὺ δ' οὐδ' ὄναρ· ἡ πολιὴ δέ
αὐτίκ' ἀναμνήσει ταῦτά σε πάντα κόμη.

XXXVI A.P. 5.97 ῾Ρουφίνου, Pl[a] τοῦ αὐτοῦ (sc. ῾Ρουφίνου)

XXXVII A.P. 5.103 ῾Ρουφίνου, Pl[a] τοῦ αὐτοῦ (sc. ῾Ρουφίνου)
[J] εἰς Προδίκην
1 Προδόκη P   σε CPl: τε ?P

[XXXVIII] A.P. 5.23 Καλλιμάχου, Pl[a] τοῦ αὐτοῦ (sc. ῾Ρουφίνου)
[J] εἰς Κωνώπιον τὴν ἑταίραν

66

[XXXIX]

εἰ τοίην χάριν εἶχε γυνὴ μετὰ Κύπριδος εὐνήν,
οὐκ ἄν τοι κόρον ἔσχεν ἀνὴρ ἀλόχοισιν ὁμιλῶν·
πᾶσαι γὰρ μετὰ Κύπριν ἀτερπέες εἰσὶ γυναῖκες.

[XXXIX] A.P. 5.77 (caret Pl) τοῦ αὐτοῦ (sc. ῾Ρουφίνου), App. B.-V. 23
ἄδηλον
[J] εἰς τὰς τῶν γυναικῶν ὁμιλίας
1 εἰ τοίνυν App. cod. V   εἶχε om. App. cod. M   2 κόρον ἔσχεν
Meineke: χρονέεσκεν codd.   ordo 3–2 in App.

COMMENTARY

Rufinus can no longer endure separation from Elpis; he will return to her from Ephesus tomorrow.

The epigram takes the form of a letter, with the conventional beginning ('Ρουφῖνος 'Ελπίδι χαίρειν) and end (ἐρρῶσθαί σε εὔχομαι). There is no other epigram of this form in the Anthology, and this epigram has nothing in common with the literary love-letter, whether of the type of Ovid's *Heroides* or of the type of Alciphron or Philostratus. The closest parallels are Dioscorides *A.P.* 12.171 = *HE* xi, a prayer to the west wind to bring back his beloved soon; Meleager 12.53 = *HE* lxvi, a message sent by ship from the Hellespont to the beloved in Cos to say that he is returning overland; and Gaetulicus *A.P.* 5.17, where the lovers are, as here, divided by the sea, and the αὔριον-motif reappears. On the relation to Strato 12.226 see Introduction, pp. 23f.

The first three couplets make the impression of a real letter which might actually be sent; in the last couplet, however, the poet has decided to 'fly' home tomorrow, so no letter will be needed. The occasion is more likely to be real than fictitious. If it is real, it follows that Rufinus' home is within a day's journey of Ephesus. As he says that in his restlessness he walks as far as the seaport Koressos, it is a fair inference that his home is overseas, and Samos is the place which immediately suggests itself; this inference is confirmed by xvii, an epigram about two harlots who prey upon men in a harbour, and the harbour named is in fact that of Samos. Jacobs[1] x 170.

1-2 'Ρουφῖνος ... χαίρειν: this is the normal way of starting a letter, as in *e.g. P. Oxy.* 1676 'Ηρκουλανὸς 'Απλωναρίωι τῆι γλυκυτάτηι καὶ τιμιωτάτηι πλεῖστα χαίρειν.

'Ελπίς is a common name in the early centuries A.D.; see the note on Maccius 9.411.4 = *PG* 2485.

δύνασαι: δύναται (P) is accepted by all the editors, but the third person is contrary to custom in letters and is here practically disproved by τῆι 'μῆι in 1 and by τὰ σά and σεῖο in the following couplet.

3-4 βαστάζω: the Lexica have no example of the metaphorical use, *put up with*; there is one in Palladas 10.99.4, μηκέτι βαστάζων ὕβριν, and the use is normal in the New Testament, *e.g.* Rev. 2.2 οὐ δύνηι βαστάσαι κακούς... ὑπομονὴν ἔχεις καὶ ἐβάστασας, John 16.12 ἔτι πολλὰ ἔχω λέγειν ὑμῖν, ἀλλ' οὐ δύνασθε βαστάζειν ἄρτι; Arndt & Gingrich *s.v.*

τὰ σ(ά): the elision is of a very rare type; S. *O.T.* 329, *El.* 1499, *Phil.* 339; Menander *Epitr.* 219 (Sandbach); not elsewhere in the Anthology. For the phrase, *cf.* Meleager 12.159.3-4 = *HE* 4564-5 ναὶ γὰρ δὴ τὰ σά, κοῦρε, τὰ καὶ κωφοῖσι λαλεῦντα | ὄμματα.

COMMENTARY: I

φιλέρημον: elsewhere this very rare compound means *loving solitude*, anon. *A.P.* 9.373.1–2, of the τέττιξ, *Lyr. Adesp.* 7.10 Powell, of ἀχώ. The φιλ-element signifies that ἐρημία is 'dear' to διαζυγίη, *separation*.

καὶ τήν: the repetition of the article is uncharacteristic and displeasing. Strato's μουνολεχεῖς κοίτας in the parallel epigram (see Introduction, p. 24) suggests κοίτην here, with μουν. διαζυγίην in apposition.

μουνολεχῆ: the Lexica have no example except those in Strato and Rufinus. The compound appears also in Peek 261.9 (I–III A.D.) and 2030.18 (II–III A.D.), where it is a term of praise, *sleeping with one husband only*, of faithful wives. In Rufinus and Strato the meaning is *having a lonely bed, i.e.* sleeping apart from the beloved.

διαζυγίην: apparently not elsewhere; διάζευξις is very rare.

5 δακρύοισι πεφυρμένος: conventional phrasing, *e.g.* Hom. *Od.* 18.173 δακρύοισι πεφυρμένη, *Il.* 24.162, *Od.* 17.103, Ap. Rhod. 3.673 δάκρυσιν ὄσσε πεφυρμένα, Strato 12.226.1 πεφυρμένος ὄμματα κλαυθμῶι.

ἢ 'πὶ Κορησσόν: a brilliant emendation by Hecker. The site of Koressos, a hill or hilly district (Strabo 14.1.20, Diodorus 14.99), was on the coast (Hdt. 5.100 πλοῖα μὲν κατέλιπον ἐν Κορησσῶι τῆς 'Εφέσου; *cf.* Xenophon *Hell.* 1.2.7, Thrasyllus, from his fleet, ὁπλίτας πρὸς τὴν Κορησσὸν ἀποβιβάσας). Diodorus *l.c.* says that it lay about 4½ miles from Ephesus, and that is about the distance from the Artemision to the coast.

Why is Koressos specified here? Perhaps because it was a seaport; Rufinus cannot make up his mind whether to stay or to leave; he goes to and fro between the centre of Ephesus and the port.

6 νηὸν... 'Αρτέμιδος: one of the three largest temples ever built by Greeks; Dinsmoor, *The architecture of ancient Greece* (3rd ed. London 1950) 127 *seqq.*, with bibliography 375 *seqq.*; Bürchner, *RE* 5.2807.

7 ἀλλά: seldom later than first in its sentence or clause; there is nothing comparable in Denniston *GP* (2nd ed. Oxford 1954) 22–3, but Callimachus *ap.* Athen. 318B = *HE* 1119 is a clear instance, Κλεινίου ἀλλὰ θυγατρὶ δίδου χάριν; so also Philodemus 11.41.7 = *PG* 3266 αὐτὴν ἀλλὰ κτλ., and Gaetulicus 5.17.5 οὖριος ἀλλ' ἐπίλαμψον.

πάτρη: this is due to the Corrector in P, whose πατρι may represent πατρίς.

δεδέξεται: Hom. *Il.* 5.238, a very rare form.

8 πτήσομαι: for 'fly' in similar contexts *cf.* Alciphron 4.18 (2.3).17 εὐθὺς πετομένη πρὸς ἡμᾶς, Philostr. *epist. amat.* 28 (47) πτηνὸς γενόμενος δεῦρο ἐλήλυθα, Lucian *dial. meretr.* 9.4 διέπτην ἐπειγόμενος ἐπὶ τοιαύτην γυναῖκα; in a letter of the second century A.D., P. Giessen 17.10–12 ὤφελον εἰ ἐδυνάμεθα πέτασθαι καὶ ἐλθεῖν καὶ προσκυνῆσαί σε.

ἐρρῶσθαι...εὐχόμενος: ἐρρῶσθαί σε εὔχομαι is not much less common than ἔρρωσο at the end of letters, but the participle εὐχόμενος is awkward here, seeming to attach the farewell-formula to the content of the letter, contrary

72

to custom and to common-sense. The incoherence is not, however, seriously confusing – 'Tomorrow I shall fly to you; wishing you good health ...'

II

Make merry, for life is short.

This is one of the commonest themes in the Anthology: Asclepiades 5.85 = *HE* ii, Thymocles 12.32 = *HE* i, Antiphanes 10.100 = *PG* vii, Apollonides 11.25 = *PG* xxvii, Argentarius 5.118 = *PG* xi and 11.28 = *PG* xxx, Strato 11.19, Palladas 11.62; *cf.* Philostratus *epist. amat.* 17 (35) and 55 (34), Tibullus 1.1.69, Hor. *Od.* 1.9.13. The phrasing is entirely Rufinus' own.

Jacobs[1] x 164, [3]v 51, Mackail xii 1.

1 πυκασώμεθα: a common verb with στεφάνοις or the like (*orac. ap.* Demosth. 21.52 κάρη στεφάνοις πυκάσαντας, Theocr. 2.153 στεφάνοισι τὰ δώματα τῆνα πυκαξεῖν, E. *Alc.* 796 στεφάνοις πυκασθείς, Hdt. 7.197.2 στέμμασι πᾶς πυκασθείς, Anacreont. 42.15–16 στεφανίσκοις | πεπυκασμένος) but very rare without some such qualification, as here, in E. *Tro.* 353 πύκαζε κρᾶτ' ἐμὸν νικηφόρον, and in Menander *Sam.* 732 πύκαζε σύ | κρᾶτα.

τὸν ἄκρατον: It was customary to pour libations of unmixed wine while invoking the name of the beloved (Callimachus 12.51.1–2 = *HE* 1063–4, Meleager 5.136.2 = *HE* 4223, 5.137.4 = *HE* 4231, Theocr. 14.18 with schol. p. 298 W.), but drinking unmixed wine was characteristic only of barbarians (Hdt. 1.207.6, Ar. *Ach.* 75, Xen. *Anab.* 4.5.27; παράλυσιν τῶν σωμάτων ποιεῖ, said Mnesitheus *ap.* Athenaeus 2.36B; see Page, *Sappho and Alcaeus* (Oxford 1955) 308) and is seldom referred to except in Comic contexts (*e.g.* Ar. *Ach.* 1229, *Equ.* 85 *seqq.*, *Eccl.* 1123, Men. *fr.* 443 K.-T., Athen. 6. 246A). Those who drink ἄκρατον do so in order to become thoroughly intoxicated, and it is unlikely that Rufinus intended this in the present context; he is saying 'let us make merry, for youth and life are short', not 'let us get hopelessly drunk'. The truth must be that ἄκρατον here means simply *wine*, a sense not recognised by LSJ but attested as early as Sophilus *fr.* 3 συνεχὴς ἄκρατος...ἴσον ἴσωι, where ἄκρατος obviously means *wine*, not *unmixed wine*, for ἴσον ἴσωι says that it was mixed with an equal part of water. Ar. *Eccl.* 1123, κέρασον ἄκρατον, looks more like an example of κεράννυμι in the sense *pour* than of ἄκρατος in the sense *wine*, though oxymoron may be intended. Ussher *ad loc.* suggests that ἄκρατος 'had perhaps even now become so common that its literal sense was little felt', and quotes Revelation 14.10, αὐτὸς πίεται ἐκ τοῦ οἴνου τοῦ θυμοῦ τοῦ θεοῦ, τοῦ κεκερασμένου ἀκράτου ἐν τῶι ποτηρίωι τῆς ὀργῆς αὐτοῦ, but there the sense is, as Arndt and Gingrich say, *the wine of God's wrath, poured unmixed into the cup of his anger*, κεκερασμένου meaning *poured* as in Revelation 18.6 and Lucillius *A.P.* 11.137.2 (a sense of the verb not recognised by LSJ).

2 ἕλκωμεν: a colloquial expression; Antiphanes *fr.* 237.2–3 δέπας...ἕλκουσι, Eubulus *fr.* 56 μάλ' ἀνδρικήν | τῶν Θηρικλείων... | εἷλκον, Ar. *Equ.* 107 ἕλχ' ἕλκε, Argentarius 11.28.3 = *PG* 1465 δέπας ἕλκε.

κύλικας μείζονας: It was customary at symposia to proceed from smaller to larger cups; Diog. Laert. 1.104 Ἕλληνες ἀρχόμενοι μὲν ἐν μικροῖς πίνουσι, πλησθέντες δὲ ἐν μεγάλοις. *Cf.* Alcaeus *fr.* 346.2 κὰδ δάερρε κυλίχναις μεγάλαις, E. *Ion* 1178–9 ἀφαρπάζειν χρεών | οἰνηρὰ τεύχη σμικρά, μεγάλα δ' ἐσφέρειν, Sophilus *fr.* 3.2 τὴν μείζον' ᾔτουν, Men. *fr.* 443 K.–T. τοῦτο δὴ τὸ νῦν ἔθος, | "ἄκρατον" ἐβόων, "τὴν μεγάλην", Alexis *fr.* 111.1 παῖ, τὴν μεγάλην δός, Athen. 6.246A τοὺς ἄλλους ἀκρατοκώθωνας καλῶν αὐτὸς τὴν μεγάλην ἔσπακεν (quoted by Headlam on Herodas 1.81); Agathias 5.289.4 ζωροτέρωι μείζονι κισσυβίωι, Hor. *epod.* 9.33 *capaciores adfer huc, puer, scyphos.*

3–4 τὰ λοιπά: either adjectival, the pleasures that lie in the future if old age did not prevent indulgence, or adverbial, with κωλύσει absolute, *will be an impediment.*

καὶ τὸ τέλος θάνατος: *sc.* κωλύσει; possibly *and, at the end, death* (τὸ τέλος adverbial as in Plato *Laws* 740E), but more probably *and the end, death.*

III

Europa's kiss reaches to the lover's soul.

A variation on the theme of Meleager 5.171 = *HE* xxxv εἴθ' ὑπ' ἐμοῖς νῦν χείλεσι χείλεα θεῖσα | ἀπνευστὶ ψυχὰν τὰν ἐν ἐμοὶ προπίοι, 'Plato' 5.78 τὴν ψυχὴν Ἀγάθωνα φιλῶν ἐπὶ χείλεσιν ἔσχον, | ἦλθε γὰρ ἡ τλήμων ὡς διαβησομένη; Prop. 1.13.17 *cupere optatis animam deponere labris.* In Meleager 12.133 = *HE* lxxxiv the lover, instead of rendering up his own soul, drinks in the soul of the beloved, φιλήσας | Ἀντίοχον ψυχῆς ἡδὺ πέπωκα μέλι.

The phrasing is as usual quite unlike that of any of the models.

Jacobs[1] x 174.

1–2 φίλαμα: this and θνατός in xxxiv 3 are the only 'Doric' alphas in Rufinus; Planudes may be right in normalising.

καὶ ἦν...κἄν: presumably co-ordinated as in Paton's translation, *though it reach only to the lips, though it but lightly touch the mouth.* This is unusually tautologous, but there is no sense in such an alternative as *quand il atteint les lèvres, ou quand il effleure seulement la bouche* (Waltz).

3 ἐρίσασα: see the Introduction, p. 41.

4 ἐξ ὀνύχων: ὄνυξ typifies the furthest extremity of the body, as in Asclepiades 5.162.2 = *HE* 843 ὁ πόνος δύεται εἰς ὄνυχα, Rhianus 12.93.10 = *HE* 3217 κὰς νεάτους ἐκ κορυφῆς ὄνυχας, Automedon 5.129.2 = *PG* 1510 ἐξ... ὀνύχων, Philip 9.709.4 = *PG* 3055 ἐκ κορυφῆς ἐς ἄκρους...ὄνυχας.

IV

Melita deserves a sculptor of the class of Praxiteles or Polyclitus. The theme has no precedent in the Anthology; that it may nevertheless have been commonplace is suggested by Plautus *Poen.* 5.4.101–2 *O Apelle, O Zeuxis pictor,* | *cur numero estis mortui, hoc exemplo ut pingeretis?*, and Philostratus *epist. amat.* 34 (65) Φειδία καὶ Λύσιππε καὶ Πολύκλειτε, ὡς ταχέως ἐπαύσασθε· οὐ γὰρ ἂν πρὸ τούτου τι ἄγαλμα ἄλλο ἐποιήσατε. Jacobs[1] x 162, [3]v 52.

2 αἱ ταῖς: this reading was probably taken by Planudes from his independent source; as a conjecture it would be far above his level.

3–4 πυρόεντα ὄμματα: the idea is commonplace (*e.g.* Meleager 5.96.1–2 = *HE* 4296–7 τὰ δ' ὄμματα, Τιμάριον, πῦρ. | ἢν ἐσίδηις, καίεις), the phrase is novel. πυρόεις does not occur in *HE*, in *PG* only of the torch of Eros, πυρόεσσα πεύκη in Alpheus *Plan.* 212.1 = *PG* 3578 and Flaccus, *Plan.* 211.3 = *PG* 3865; *cf.* anon. *A.P.* 9.132.3 πυρόεις πόθος.

The difference in style between Rufinus and the *Cycle* is epitomised in the contrast between πυρόεντα ὄμματα and φλογόεσσαν ὀπωπήν, which means much the same thing, in Paulus 5.221.1.

δειρῆς φέγγος: a striking phrase, as if Melita were a divinity (*cf.* 6 ὡς μακάρων ξοάνωι); *cf. H. Dem.* 278 φέγγος ἀπὸ χροὸς ἀθανάτοιο | λάμπε θεᾶς, Bacchylides 17.102 ἀπὸ γὰρ ἀγλαῶν λάμπε γυίων σέλας ὥστε πυρός (of the Nereids).

V

The slave-girl preferred to the luxurious lady.

The preference-motif is common in the Anthology (*e.g.* Meleager 12.86 = *HE* xviii, son preferred to mother; Philodemus 12.173 = *PG* xvi, maiden preferred to courtesan; Argentarius 5.89 = *PG* iv, plain girl preferred to beauty), but this variation has its closest parallel in Horace *sat.* 1.2.78 *seqq.*, 127 *seqq.*; *cf.* Strato 12.192. Agathias, 5.302.15–18, disapproves of connections with θεραπαινίδες.

Jacobs[1] x 149–50, [2]xiii 65, [3]v 65; Hecker 1843, 29–30.

1 σοβαρῶν: see the Introduction, pp. 44ff.

δουλίδας: the form is rare, and there seems to have been some objection to it; Pollux 3.74 δουλίς, Ὑπερείδηι (*fr.* 235) εἰρημένον, οὐκ ἐπαινετόν. The Lexica cite nothing beyond Hyperides, Rufinus, and *IG* 14.1839.8, II–III A.D.; add Herodas 7.126, with Headlam's note, and Peek 309.3, I–II A.D.

2 σπατάλοις: see the Introduction, pp. 46f.

κλέμμασι: for κλέμμα, κλέπτω, of furtive love, *cf.* Strato 12.21.1, Paulus

5.219.1, 5.221.1, Aelian *N.A.* 1.2 δυσέρωτες ἄνθρωποι φίλημα ἢ κνίσμα θηρώμενοι ἤ τι ἄλλο κλέμμα ἐρωτικόν. The noun is not in *HE*, nor in any amatory context in *PG*.

3 φρύαγμα: the snort of the superior person, metaphorical already in Menander *fr.* 333; Meleager 12.33.3 = *HE* 4482 μὴ γαῦρα φρυάσσου, 12.101.3 = *HE* 4532 τὸ δ' ὑπ' ὀφρύσι κεῖνο φρύαγμα, Agathias 5.282.5 φρύαγμα τὸ παιδικόν, 10.64.1 ποῦ τὸ φρύαγμα;, Alciphron *Epist. agr.* 2.24 (3.27).2 σὺ δὲ φρυάττηι, Mesomedes 3.3 (Heitsch) κοῦφα φρυάγματα θνατῶν, Aelian, *N.A.* 7.12 μέγα φρονείτωσαν...καὶ τὸ φρύαγμα αἱρέτωσαν, Philostr. *imag.* 2.2.2 θυμοειδὲς φρύαγμά ἐστι μὲν ἤδη τῶι παιδί, Aristaenetus 2.12 φρύαγμα ὁμοζύγου πλουσίας.

4 On the apparent hiatus at mid-pentameter, see the Introduction, p. 31, whence it will appear that this phenomenon is very rare in elegiac verse at all times and extremely rare in elegant verse; in Rufinus, it is not to be accepted if easily avoidable. Some have attacked ἑσπομένη, and it may be admitted that 'following' seems hardly the *mot juste*, but such alternatives as κλεπτομένη (Dübner) and τερπομένη (Desrousseaux) are palaeographically most improbable. The likeliest solution is the insertion of θ'; it might easily be dropped by a corrector, or even by a copyist, who did not understand that καί is not continuative but stressing, 'and (θ') intercourse following even (καὶ) to the point of peril'. Nor would an emphatic γε be out of place here.

σύνοδος: see the Introduction, p. 48.

6 This line seems hopelessly corrupt. ἀλεγίζομαι (presumably middle for active *metri gratia*) cannot govern the dative case. σπατάλης (apogr.) is required, and ἐκ might be a corruption of καί (Heinsius), but then δώρων (Brunck) must replace δώροις, and that is a very unlikely change. A possible solution is to connect δώροις with ἕτοιμον, *their bed is ready for gifts, and cares nothing for luxury*, but ἕτοιμος is not so used elsewhere, and though it would be good sense to say that the slave is readily bribed whereas the proud lady needs luxurious presents, the context suggests rather a contrast of 'no gifts' and 'luxurious gifts'. T. W. Lumb, *Notes on the Greek Anthology* (London 1920) 8, suggested οὐ δελεαζόμενον, and this could be combined with δώροις ἐκ σπατάλης, *not lured by gifts from luxury*. He might have quoted in support *Daphnis and Chloe* 3.15 ἐπεθύμησεν ἐραστὴν κτήσασθαι δώροις δελεάσασα, but the change is not a likely one, and ἐκ σπατάλης is unconvincing.

7 προέκρινεν: see the Introduction, p. 43.

VI

Girls preferred to boys.

The theme is commonplace; *e.g.* Meleager 5.208 = *HG* ix, 12.41 = *HE* xciv, anon. *A.P.* 12.145 = *HE* viii, Argentarius 5.116 = *PG* x, anon *A.P.* 12.17, Agathias 5.278 and 10.68, Eratosthenes 5.277; *cf.* Ach. Tat. 2.35. Jacobs¹ x 162–3.

1 παιδομανής: first in Alex. Aetol. *fr.* 5.5 Powell; Meleager 5.208.1 = *HE* 4046 οὔ μοι παιδομανὴς κραδία, Agathias 5.302.8.

2 θηλυμανής: *cf.* Meleager 9.16.2 = *HE* 4387 θηλυμανεῖς Πόθοι, Antimachus *A.P.* 9.321.4 (= *fr. dub.* 149.4 Wyss), *making women mad*, Alciphron 1.6.4 λαγνός εἰμι καὶ θηλυμανής.

δίσκος ... κρόταλον: boys played with the discus; Lucian *dial. deor.* 16 (14).2 δισκεύειν ἐμάνθανε ('Υάκινθος), κἀγὼ ('Απόλλων) συνεδίσκευον αὐτῶι. κρόταλον is especially the instrument of girls who entertained at symposia; *cf.* Meleager 5.175.8 = *HE* 4361, Dioscorides 11.195.4 = *HE* 1694, Antimachus *l.c.* κροτάλων θηλυμανεῖς ὄτοβοι, Thyillus *A.P.* 7.223.1 ἡ κροτάλοις ὀρχηστρίς, Macedonius 5.271.1–2 τήν ποτε...χρυσέωι κροτάλωι σειομένην σπατάλην.

latet spurci aliquid, said Paton, inscrutably.

3–4 ἀδόλου: in a similar context, Philostr. *epist. amat.* 22 (40) ἐκ φυκίου δολερὸν ἄνθος, and later ἐν ταῖς ἀδόλως καλαῖς. The word is not in *HE* or *PG*.

γύψου χρώματα: γύψος is *creta*, chalk, a Roman cosmetic; Ovid *A.A.* 3.199–200, Hor. *epod.* 12.10, Martial 6.93.9, 8.33.17, Cic. *fam.* 7.6.1 (for actors' hands); *cf.* Hdt. 7.69, 8.27; *RE* 7.2092. The Greek cosmetic to produce whiteness was ψιμύθιον (white lead; Ussher on Ar. *Eccl.* 878). χρίσματα (Pl) is not likely to be corruption or conjecture. As Dr Dawe observes, it implies the use of *creta* in the form of paste; I have not seen any other evidence of this. The plural perhaps covers various shades of white colour.

φύκους ἄνθος: *cf.* Philostr. *l.c.* ἐκ φυκίου ἄνθος, Lucianus 11.408.5, Macedonius 11.370.2 τὴν νοθοκαλλοσύνην φύκεῖ χριομένην; a preparation from seaweed for producing red colouring. See Gow on Theocr. 15.16.

In general, women made their complexions white with ψιμύθιον (white lead) or κηρωτή, *cerussa* (wax-salve) or γύψος, *creta*, chalk; or red with φῦκος (seaweed), ἔγχουσα (alkanet), or νίτρον (soda). All these except γύψος appear, with others, in the catalogue in Aristophanes *fr.* 320; *cf.* Pollux 5.95 *seqq.* I have not noticed the cosmetic use of γύψος in a strictly Greek context.

ἐπεισόδιον: substantival in Crinagoras 6.232.6 = *PG* 2019. The φύκους ἄνθος is 'episodic' in the sense that it is an artificial addition to beauty, contrasted with the ἄδολος χρὼς of the boy; the translators paraphrase, *that are laid on* (Paton), *emprunté* (Waltz), *geliehene* (Beckby).

5–6 Variation on a common theme; *cf.* Archilochus *fr.* 122.5–9 (δελφῖνες and θῆρες change places), Verg. *ecl.* 1.59 (*cervi* and *pisces*), Hor. *A.P.* 30 (*delphines* and *apri*), *od.* 1.2.7 *seqq.* (*piscium genus* and *dammae*), *epod.* 16.34 *ametque salsa levis hircus aequora.*

δενδροκόμης: here only; -όκομος E. *Hel.* 1107, Ar. *Nub.* 280.

VII

The revenge of the passing years on a proud beauty.

There are several variations on this theme: (*a*) as here, age has taken revenge, Rufinus IX, XXX, XXXVII, Macedonius 5.271, Agathias 5.273; (*b*) a warning that old age will come, or a prayer that it may come soon, Rufinus XXXIII, Macedonius 5.233, Julianus 5.298; (*c*) old age has come but beauty remains, Rufinus XIX with examples in Pref.; (*d*) love resisted in youth, sought in age, Paulus 5.234; (*e*) especially in paederastic epigrams, the growth of hair (see X Pref.).

On the relation of this epigram to Ausonius *ep.* 34, see the Introduction, p. 21; to Strato 12.226, p. 24.

Rufinus' treatment of the theme is conventional, his phraseology distinctive as usual.

Jacobs[1] x 175–6, [3]v 53.

1 οὐκ ἔλεγον: *cf.* Meleager 12.132 'ι = *PG* 4104 οὔ σοι ταῦτ' ἐβόων, Philodemus 5.107.5 = *PG* 3192 τοῦτ' ἐβόων αἰεὶ καὶ προύλεγον.

προεφώνουν: see the Introduction, p. 43.

2 αἱ διαλυσίφιλοι: *sc.* τρίχες (πολιαί). On the form of the adjective (here only) see the Introduction, p. 5.

3 σῶμα ῥακῶδες: *cf.* Ar. *Plut.* 1065 ὄψει κατάδηλα τοῦ προσώπου τὰ ῥάκη, Crinagoras 7.380.6–7 = *PG* 2004–5 τὠλιγηπελὲς ῥάκος | Εὐνικίδαο, σήπεται δ' ὑπὸ σποδῶι, Antiphilus 9.242.5 = *PG* 905 βίου ῥάκος, of an old man, anon. (ascribed to Antiphilus) 11.66.1–2 = *PG* 1095–6 ῥακόεντα...χρῶτα, Lucian *merc. cond.* 39 τὸ ἀκμαιότατον τοῦ σώματος ἐπιτρίψας καὶ ῥάκος σε πολυσχιδὲς ἐργασάμενος.

5–6 μετέωρε: no other poet of any period uses this adjective in this sense, *haughty*, though μετάρσιος is so used occasionally from Euripides (*Andr.* 1220) to Agathias (5.273.1). In prose the use appears first in Polybius (3.82.2) and is rare thereafter: Lucian *Nigr. init.* ὡς σεμνὸς ἡμῖν σφόδρα καὶ μετέωρος ἐπανελήλυθας, 5 γαῦρος καὶ μετέωρος, Philostr. *epist. amat.* 38 (68) ὑψηλόν τε ὁρᾶις καὶ μετέωρος βαδίζεις; in Julian *Misop.* 361A, ἐπαρθέντες τὸν νοῦν καὶ μετέωροι, the uncomplimentary colour is watered down, rather *uplifted* than *high and mighty*, though (as in Philostratus) the tone is ironical.

ὡς δὲ τάφον: *cf.* Lucian *Timon* 5 ὥσπερ τινὰ στήλην παλαιοῦ νεκροῦ... παρέρχονται.

VIII

Rufinus a willing slave of Boöpis.
There is no other epigram in the Anthology much like this one. The vocabulary is distinctive.
Jacobs¹ x 176–8, ³v 67.

1 λάτριν: the idea is commonplace, the word rare in such contexts; anon. *A.P.* 5.100.1–2 λάτρις Ἔρωτος | φοιτῶ, Paulus 5.283.6–7 Ἐρώτων | λάτρις. **γλυκύδωρος**: thrice in Bacchylides, not elsewhere.

2 ταῦρον ὑποζεύξας: the image is suggested by the name Βοῶπις. The ζυγὸν of Love is a commonplace; see Gow on Theocr. 12.15. **αὐτόμολον**: usually *deserting*, here *coming of one's own accord*, as in Honestus 9.250.4 = *PG* 2425 πέτροι αὐτόμολοι, of the walls of Thebes, Opp. *Hal.* 3.360 κλητοί τ' αὐτόμολοί τε.

3 αὐτοθελῆ: a very rare word; Meleager 7.470.6 = *HE* 4735, Honestus 11.45.1 = *PG* 2436, Leonides Alex. *A.P.* 9.79.1. **πάνδουλον**: elsewhere only Manetho 4.602 πανδούλους...ὁμόζυγα λατρεύοντας. **αὐτοκέλευστον**: Xen. *Anab.* 3.4.5 and occasionally in prose thereafter.

4 *Cf.* Irenaeus 5.249.4 κεῖμαι ἐλευθερίης οὐκ ἐπιδευόμενος.

5 φίλης: neither *dear* nor *my own* seems appropriate. There is a close parallel to this apparently meaningless φίλος in *A.P.* 5.2.4, on which see the Introduction, p. 5, and there are one or two more distantly comparable examples in Hom. *Il.* 2.261 εἰ μὴ ἐγώ σε λαβὼν ἀπὸ μὲν φίλα εἵματα δύσω, and Theocritus 21.20 τοὺς δ' ἁλιεῖς ἤγειρε φίλος πόνος, where *carus* is excluded by the contexts and *proprius* is pointless.

Jacobs' conjecture φίλη has not found much favour; the lateness of the vocative in the sentence is against it, and so is its position between ἄχρι and πολιῆς, though the use of the vocative φίλη late in the epigram is in itself characteristic of the style (Rufinus XXVI 4, Paulus 5.254.5 and 5.255.17, Cometas 5.265.3).

IX

Age's revenge on the proud beauty; see VII Pref.
Jacobs¹ x 179–81, ²XIII 67, ³v 55; Hecker 1843, 30–1; 1852, 203–4.

1–2 Μέλισσα: first attested as the name of the tyrant Periander's wife; see the note on Argentarius 5.32.1 = *PG* 1307. **χρύσεα...κάλλεα**: χρύσεος here = *bright, shining*; see XIX 1 n. **περίοπτα**: a word common in prose, not in poetry (= περίβλεπτα, XII 3). **πολυθρυλήτου**: prose, from Plato *Rep.* 556B to Julian *Misop.* 352A.

79

φαντασίης: a very rare word in poetry, usually *imagination, idea*, or the like, as in Macedonius 5.235.2, Agathias 1.34.4, Damocharis *Plan.* 310.4. It is common especially in philosophy (Diog. Laert. 4.53, 5.29; Stoic term, 6.70 *seqq.*, 7.45; Epicurean, 10.80). Here *appearance* as in Aristot. *meteor.* 339a35 τοῦ γάλακτος φαντασία, Athen. 5.212c ἐπ' ἀργυρόποδος κατακοιμίζεται φορείου καὶ πορφυρῶν στρωμάτων...οὐδενὸς οὐδὲ 'Ρωμαίων ἐν τοιαύτηι φαντασίαι καταχλιδῶντος τῆς 'Αττικῆς; not *face*, but *appearance* more generally – *de sumptuoso apparatu*, as Jacobs says.

3 ὀφρύες: the word may stand, without any qualification, for *gravity* (*cf.* Antipater of Sidon 7.409.2 = *HE* 639, Strato 12.2.6 τούτοις ὀφρύες οὐκ ἔπρεπον, Alciphron 4.7 (1.34).1 σεμνός τις ἐγένου καὶ τὰς ὀφρῦς ὑπὲρ τοὺς κροτάφους ἐπῆρας), and often connotes *haughtiness* (Meleager 12.101.3 = *HE* 4542 τὸ δ' ὑπ' ὀφρύσι κεῖνο φρύαγμα, Parmenion 9.43.3 = *PG* 2594, Lucillius 10.122.3, Strato 12.186.1, Paulus 5.300.1, Agathias 5.299.5).

γαῦρα: *cf.* Meleager 12.33.3 = *HE* 4482 μὴ γαῦρα φρυάσσου, whence Jacobs conjectured γαῦρα φρυάγματα here.

μέγας αὐχήν: the proud person's neck is usually *high*; ὑψαύχην Paulus 5.300.1, Agathias 9.641.1, Irenaeus 5.251.5, Claudian *Ruf.* 1.53 *alta cervice vagatur*; so here μέγας = *long*, implying *high*.

4 σοβαρῶν: see the Introduction, pp. 44ff.

ταρσῶν: *ankles*; the χρυσοφόρος σπατάλη means or implies golden ornaments, here plainly anklets. σπατάλη itself may mean *bracelet*, but it would be characteristic of Rufinus to say *gold-bearing luxury of the ankles*, meaning ankles adorned with golden bracelets.

5 ψαφαρή τε κόμην: *cf.* Nonnus *D.* 4.363 ψαφαρή...χαίτη.

παχεῖα: a poet who pronounces ἐρίσασα has no right to complain if τρᾶχεῖα is ascribed to him; but τραχεῖα γυνή is a *shrew*, a bad-tempered woman (*e.g.* Xanthippe in Diog. Laert. 2.37), and that notion is not well suited to a context concerned with the contrasts of wealth and poverty, youth and age. περὶ ποσσὶ παχεῖα recalls Archilochus *fr.* 206 περὶ σφυρὸν παχεῖα μισητὴ γυνή, and the contrast of thick ankles in old age with the χρυσοφόρος σπατάλη of her ankles in her prime is appropriate. For the corruption *cf.* Ach. Tat. 4.3.5, where Hercher corrected τραχὺ to παχύ.

τ' ἀχρεία for τραχεῖα was suggested by Hecker (ψαφαρή τε κόμην περὶ ποσσί τ', ἀχρεία), but it makes the line jerky, and one expects a more explicit characteristic than ἀχρεία provides (*good-for-nothing*, Diog. Laert. 2.81 and occasionally in the New Testament; the form ἀχρείη would have suited the dialect better).

6 τέρματα: these are the ends to which luxurious courtesans come.

παλλακίδων: the form παλλακὶς appears in Homer but very seldom afterwards.

X

A boy, reaching manhood, no longer sought by lovers.
Variation on a very common theme (*e.g.* Asclepiades 12.36 = *HE* xlvi,
Alcaeus 12.30 = *HE* viii, Meleager 12.33 = *HE* xc, anon. 12.40 and
12.39 = *HE* xii and xxxii, Automedon 11.326 = *PG* x, Diocles 12.35 =
PG iv, Strato 12.182, 186, 204); in most of these the change in the boy is
related to the growth of unwanted hair, in Rufinus to the cutting of long
hair on passing from boyhood to manhood.

The name of the boy is not given. The omission is quite common in the
Anthology when the person is directly addressed as here and in xiv, xvi,
xxiii and xxvi; much rarer where the subject is referred to in the third
person as in Diodorus 5.122.1–2 = *PG* 2106–7 n., and in Rufinus xix
(apparently) and xxx.

Jacobs[1] x 181–2, [3]v 64.

1 "χαῖρε" λέγεις: a common motif in this sort of of context; *cf.* Diocles
12.35.1 = *PG* 2096 "χαῖρε" ποτ' οὐκ εἰπόντα, Strato 12.186.2 μηδὲ τὸ
"χαῖρε" λέγων, Rufinus xxxiii 1–2.

ἀπῆλθεν: *depart* may signify *die* (*e.g.* anon. *A.P.* 11.335.1 καὶ ἐν ζωοῖς καὶ
ἀπελθών), but here the sense is probably *your complexion has disappeared*. This
couplet implies the emergence of facial hair, the next couplet refers to the
hair of the head.

2 λύγδου: a variety of Parian marble famed for its whiteness; *cf.* Asclepiades
5.194.3–4 = *HE* 970–1 οἷά τε λύγδου | γλυπτήν, Philodemus 5.13.3 = *PG*
3168 τὰ λύγδινα κώνια μαστῶν, Rufinus xix 3 δειρὴ λυγδινέη, Anacreont.
15.27 περὶ λυγδίνωι τραχήλωι, Hor. *od.* 1.19.5–6 *urit me Glycerae nitor* |
fulgentis Pario marmore purius.

βάσκανε: the usual sense *spiteful, malicious*, is possible here (as in the only
places where the word occurs in *HE* and *PG*, Erinna 7.712.3 = *HE* 1791,
Leonidas 7.13.4 = *HE* 2566, Antiphanes 9.256.3–4 = *PG* 744), but *be-
witcher, charmer*, may be preferred, as in Alciphron *epist. parasit.* 3.26 (62).2
μοιχὸς πολιορκεῖ τὴν οἰκίαν, ὁ 'Ηλεῖος νεανίσκος, εἷς τῶν 'Ολυμπίασι
βασκάνων.

λειότερον: for λεῖος of a *smooth* (= hairless) boy, *cf. e.g.* Strato 12.222.1.

3 προσπαίζεις: of affectionate jesting as in Alciphron *epist. parasit.* 3.2 (5).1
συμβαλών μοι...χρηστῶς ἠσπάσατο...καὶ μικρὰ προσπαίξας κτλ., 3.29
(65).3 προσπαίζειν τε γλαφυρὸς καὶ λαλῆσαι στωμύλος, Ach. Tat. 2.20.2
βουλόμενος αὐτὸν εἰς φιλίαν ἀγαγεῖν προσέπαιζε πολλάκις...καὶ ἔσκωπτε
...σὺν γέλωτι, Lucian *dial. meretr.* 12.1 ἄρτι μὲν Λυκαίνηι προσέπαιζες
ἐμοῦ ὁρώσης, ὡς λυποίης ἐμέ, *Demonax* 21 ἐγέλα τὰ πολλὰ καὶ τοῖς ἀνθρώποις
προσέπαιζε; Diog Laert. (4.61, 7.164) uses this verb of his satirical epigrams.
The word is not in *HE* or *PG* and is very rare in amatory contexts. It usually
implies joking at someone's expense.

τρίχας ἠφάνικας: on the ceremonial cutting of the hair, and of the first beard, at the end of a boy's seventeenth year, see Marquardt *Privatleben der Römer* (2nd ed. Leipzig 1879) 581; the custom appears to have entered Rome from Greece early in the imperial period. The theme of these lines is elaborately treated in Philostratus *epist. amat.* 16 (26), ὦ ἀνδροφόνε τῆς κεφαλῆς, τί ἔδει μαχαιρῶν ἐπὶ τὰς τρίχας;...οἷον θέρος ἐξέκοψας κτλ., 58 (61) μελέτω σοι τῶν βοστρύχων, ὡς τοὺς μὲν ταῖς παρειαῖς συγκαταβαίνειν ἠρέμα, τοὺς δὲ τοῖς ὤμοις ἐπικαθῆσθαι κτλ.

4 σοβαροῖς: see the Introduction, pp. 44ff.

αὐχέσι: the plural, of one person's neck, is very rare; *S. fr.* 659.4 Pearson, Apollonides 7.233.2 = *PG* 1238, Philip 9.56.4 = *PG* 2882.

πλαζομένας: the hair *strays, wanders*, over the neck; an original and lively touch of colour.

5 μετέωρε: see VII 5–6 n.

XI

A beauty-competition.

The theme of XI and XII, unique in the Anthology, is drawn from life of the kind enjoyed by the *al fresco* party in Alciphron 4.14 (1.39).4 δεινή τις φιλονεικία κατέσχε Θρυαλλίδα καὶ Μυρρίνην ὑπὲρ τῆς πυγῆς ποτέρα κρείττω καὶ ἀπαλωτέραν ἐπιδείξει. καὶ πρώτη Μυρρίνη τὸ ζωνίον λύσασα...δι' αὐτοῦ τρέμουσαν οἷόν τι μελίπηκτον γάλα τὴν ὀσφῦν ἀνεσάλευσεν, ὑποβλέπουσα εἰς τοὐπίσω πρὸς τὰ κινήματα τῆς πυγῆς. ἠρέμα δ' οἷον ἐνεργοῦσά τι ἐρωτικὸν ὑπεστέναξεν...οὐ μὴν ἀπεῖπέ γε ἡ Θρυαλλὶς ἀλλὰ τῆι ἀκολασίαι παρευδοκίμησεν αὐτήν. "οὐ γὰρ διὰ παραπετασμάτων ἐγώ" φησίν "ἀγωνίσομαι, οὐδὲ ἀκκιζομένη, ἀλλ' οἷον ἐν γυμνικῶι. καὶ γὰρ οὐ φιλεῖ προφάσεις ἀγών." ἀπεδύσατο τὸ χιτώνιον καὶ μικρὸν ὑποσιμώσασα τὴν ὀσφῦν "ἰδού, σκόπει τὸ χρῶμα" φησίν "ὡς ἄκρηβες, Μυρρίνη, ὡς ἀκήρατον, ὡς καθαρόν, τὰ παραπόρφυρα τῶν ἰσχίων ταυτί, τὴν ἐπὶ τοὺς μηροὺς ἔγκλισιν, τὸ μήτε ὑπέρογκον αὐτῶν μήτε ἄσαρκον, τοὺς γελασίνους ἐπ' ἄκρων. ἀλλ' οὐ τρέμει, νὴ Δία", ἅμ' ὑπομειδιῶσα, "ὥσπερ ἡ Μυρρίνης." καὶ τοσοῦτον παλμὸν ἐξειργάσατο τῆς πυγῆς, καὶ ἅπασαν αὐτὴν ὑπὲρ τὴν ὀσφῦν τῆιδε καὶ τῆιδε ῥέουσαν περιεδίνησεν, ὥστε ἀνακροτῆσαι πάσας καὶ νίκην ἀναπεφήνασθαι τῆς Θρυαλλίδος. ἐγένοντο δὲ καὶ περιάλλων συγκρίσεις καὶ περὶ μασταρίων ἀγῶνες.

Rufinus' epigram is very like this in spirit; the occasion is as likely to be real as fictitious. Compare also the competition described in Athenaeus 12.554c, giving the story behind the foundation of the temple of Ἀφροδίτη Καλλίπυγος: a farmer's two daughters φιλονικήσασαί ποτε πρὸς ἑαυτὰς προελθοῦσαι ἐπὶ τὴν λεωφόρον διεκρίνοντο ποτέρα εἴη καλλιπυγοτέρα κτλ.

The vocabulary and phrasing are elaborate.

Jacobs[1] x 150–3.

2 γυμνῶν: an easy change, and probably necessary, for the transferred epithet is not in the style of Rufinus.

ἀστεροπὴν μελέων: a striking phrase; the metaphor is more readily applied to the eyes, as in S. *fr.* 474.2 Pearson, Asclepiades 5.153.4 = *HE* 823 βλέμματος ἀστεροπαί, Meleager 12.110.1 = *HE* 4550 ἤστραψε γλυκὺ κάλλος.

3 καί ῥ': ἄρα, ἄρα, ἤ ῥα are common, but ῥα in other circumstances is very rare in the later epigrammatists; καί ῥα Agathias 9.677.5, anon. 11.125.3, Paulus 5.255.7 and 300.5, τούς ῥα Leontius 9.650.3, ὅς ῥα Christodorus 7.697.1.

τροχαλοῖς: normally *running* as in Palladas 7.681.3, here *round* as in Nic. *Ther.* 589.

σφραγιζομένη: *marked*, as in Philip *Plan.* 25.4 = *PG* 3069, of an athlete, ψάμμος πεσόντος νῶτον οὐκ ἐσφράγισεν.

γελασίνοις: *dimples*, of the buttocks as in Alciphron *l.c.* (Pref.); of the cheeks, Martial 7.25.6.

4 εὐαφίηι elsewhere only Agathias 5.294.16; εὐάφεια prose only and rare.

The meaning is that her buttocks were marked with round dimples; they were white and soft to the touch (literally *she bloomed with white softness-to-touch from the buttocks*).

5-6 διαιρομένης: apparently *when she separated* (her legs), *i.e.* stood with legs apart, but the verb is not so used elsewhere.

φοινίσσετο: *became red*; *cf.* Ach. Tat. 1.4.3, of the complexion, τὸ λευκὸν εἰς μέσον ἐφοινίσσετο = *the white shaded into red*; Musaeus 58–9 ἄκρα δὲ χιονέων φοινίσσετο κύκλα παρειῶν | ὡς ῥόδον ἐκ καλύκων διδυμόχροον; Asclepiades 5.203.4 = *HE* 835 μηρὸς ἐφοινίχθη.

χιονέη σάρξ: for the adjective (not in *HE*; in *PG* only Apollonides 9.244.2 = 1210 χιόνεαι νιφάδες) used of the skin *cf.* Bion 1.10 χιονέας κατὰ σαρκός, Paulus 5.246.1–2 γυίων | ...χιονέων, anon. 5.84.2 στήθεσι χιονέοις, Peek 746.3 (III–IV A.D.) χιονέοις...προσώποις.

μᾶλλον ἐρυθροτέρη: *cf.* Nicarchus 11.251.1–2 πολὺ μᾶλλον...κωφότερος.

The meaning is that when she spread her legs the colour of her skin showed a change from white to red, *i.e.* what now appeared was red, whereas what had been shown before was white.

7-8 γαληνιόωσα: in this epic form, also anon. 9.208.2.

χαράσσετο: ταράσσετο Salmasius, not without reason, for χαράσσεσθαι normally implies *breaking of a surface* (especially of the surface of the sea by oars, *Orph. Arg.* 372, 701, Nonnus *D.* 3.46, Agathias 10.14.1–2 after Antipater of Sidon 10.2.1–2 = *HE* 439), whereas Rufinus is thinking of a smooth unbroken surface. But ταράσσετο suits γαληνιόωσα no better than χαράσσετο does, and the truth probably is that χαράσσετο here means no more than *creased*.

κύματι κωφῶι: from Hom. *Il.* 14.16, where the scholia B and L explain κωφῶι as ἀφώνωι, μηδέπω παφλάζοντι; cf. *Et. Mag. s.v.*, ἀψόφωι καὶ μηδένα ἦχον ἀποτελοῦντι; the *dumb* wave of a swell as opposed to the noisy wave of a breaker.

The meaning is that her skin is like the surface of a sea which is calm (γαληνιόωσα) but creased (χαράσσετο) by the soundless wave of a swell, *i.e.* her flesh is gently rippling. *Cf.* Alciphron *l.c.* (Pref.) ὥσπερ ῥέουσαν (τὴν πυγὴν) περιεδίνησεν.

αὐτομάτη κτλ: *sponte delicata cute palpitans* (Dübner).

σαλευομένη: *cf.* Dioscorides 5.54.4 = *HE* 1500; the verb is commoner of inebriated persons, as in Leonidas *Plan.* 306.1 = *HE* 2151, Meleager 5.175.6 = *HE* 4359.

9–10 τὰς προτέρας: *sc.* Paris' former subjects for judgement, the three goddesses contrasted with ταύτας, these three women.

XII

Another beauty-competition; see XI Pref.

Jacobs[1] x 153–5, [2]XIII 65, [4]*Addenda* (Praef.) p. xxxiii; Hecker 1843, 33–4.

1 'Ροδόπη, the name in Paulus 5.219, 5.228, Irenaeus 5.249.

Μελίτη: Archias 6.39.2 = *PG* 3621, Eratosthenes 5.242, Agathias 5.282; Μελίτεια in Leonidas 6.288.1 = *HE* 2213.

'Ροδόκλεια: Leontius *Plan.* 283.

2 μηριόνην: here only = *feminal*; *cf.* Antipater of Sidon 12.97.2 = *HE* 633, Strato 12.247.6.

3 περίβλεπτοι: Antipater of Sidon 9.151.1 = *HE* 568, Meleager 5.184.5 = *HE* 4374, Automedon 12.34.5 = *PG* 1579, Strato 12.213.1.

4 νέκταρι λειβόμεναι: λειπόμεναι cannot stand (*hoc unum illis deerat, quod nondum nectare vescebantur*, Jacobs; *tantum nectar deerat* Hecker, comparing Aristaen. 1.2 μόνωι γε τῶι ἀριθμῶι λειπόμεναι τῶν Χαρίτων). *Dripping with nectar* implies that they had anointed themselves with a divinely scented unguent, like the Nereids in Alcaeus 7.1.3 = *HE* 64 νέκταρι... Νηρηΐδες ἐχρίσαντο; in Nossis 6.275.3 = *HE* 2809 Samytha dedicates to Aphrodite a hair-net which ἁδύ τι νέκταρος ὄσδει. νεκτάρεος = *fragrant* already in Homer, of the garments of mortals, *Il.* 3.385, 18.25. νέκταρ ἀλειφόμεναι, the conjecture of Salmasius, deserves consideration, but the tense should be aorist, and the change will then be less probable.

5–6 πολύτιμος: Waltz and Beckby translate as if this were a noun, *precious jewel*; it is, however, an adjective (as it happens, a very rare one), and needs a noun. It makes no sense with ῥοδών, nor can μέσος μηρῶν be treated as a noun equivalent to μηριόνης; μέσος supports πολύτιμος in its demand for a noun, and adds that the noun must be masculine. That noun must have stood in the following line; and, as it is obvious that two lines describing Melita are missing, it it is hardly less obvious that the gap follows 5, not 6 as editors generally suppose. The objection that ῥοδών will then fall within the description of Melita, not of ῾Ροδόπη, weighs very light in the scale.

ῥοδών: the word is chosen for the context; Hesych. *s.v.* ῥοδών· Μιτυληναῖοι τὸ τῆς γυναικός, schol. Theocr. 11.10 p. 242 W. τὸ γυναικεῖον μόριον καὶ ῥόδον καὶ ῥοδωνιάν φασιν, ὡς Κρατῖνος ἐν Νεμέσει (*fr.* 109); *cf.* Pherecr. *fr.* 108.29.

†πολιῶι†: the adjective is nonsense with ζεφύρωι in this context. πολλῶι (Hecker, comparing Euenus 11.49.5 = *PG* 2328, Zelotus 9.31.2 πολύς... νότος) is inappropriate; ἁπαλῶι (Jacobs) is not a likely change; λείωι (*i.e.* λίωι, expanded to πολιῶι; Jacobs) is not a good epithet for a *cutting* wind.

σχιζόμενος: it seems natural to talk of a *cutting* wind, but a parallel in Greek is hard to find.

7 ὑάλωι ἴσος: *cf.* XIX 1 ὑαλόεσσα παρειή (where LSJ render *glass-coloured*), Strato 12.249.2 παιδὸς ἐφ' ὑαλέην ὄψιν; *ad laevitatem referendum est*, said Jacobs, but the reference may be to the colour (*cf.* Leonidas 6.211.3 = *HE* 1961 μηλοῦχον ὑαλόχροα) or possibly the transparency of the skin. ἴσος agrees either with μηριόνης or with the masculine noun lost in the gap.

ὑγρομέτωπος: here only. The element -μέτωπος suggests that ὑγρο- means rather *soft* than *moist*; for ὑγρός, of the eyes, *melting, languishing*, see the note on Leonidas Plan. 396.3 = *HE* 2153 and the examples cited in LSJ *s.v.* II 5.

8 πρωτογλυφές: here only. The phrase recalls Theocritus 9.437.2 = *HE* 3475 ἀρτιγλυφὲς ξόανον. For the failure of γλ to lengthen a preceding short vowel, see the note on Leonidas 6.293.1 = *HE* 2301. πρωτο- is not *first* but *newly*, as in πρωτοπαγής (Hom. *Il.* 5.194, 24.267).

It is very extraordinary that a couplet from Rufinus XXI should have been interpolated in P between 7–8 and 9–10.

9–10 For the motif, *cf.* Diog. Laert. 2.67 Διονυσίου δέ ποτε τριῶν ἑταιρῶν οὐσῶν μίαν ἐκλέξασθαι κελεύσαντος, τὰς τρεῖς ἀπήγαγεν (ὁ ᾽Αρίστιππος) εἰπὼν "οὐδὲ τῶι Πάριδι συνήνεγκε μίαν προκρῖναι."

XIII

Woman should be neither very thin nor very fat.

This is the feeblest of Rufinus' epigrams: *don't embrace the very thin or the very fat, because the one has not enough flesh and the other has too much*. It is a variation on a common theme: *e.g.* Honestus 5.20 = *PG* i, neither very young nor very old; Philodemus 12.173 = *PG* xvi, the too willing and the too reluctant; Rufinus xv; Alciphron *fr.* 5, of Lais, οὔτε κατάξηρος οὔτε κατάσαρκος; Martial 11.100 *habere amicam nolo, Flacce, subtilem* | ... | *sed idem amicam nolo mille librarum*; in Alciphron, quoted in XI Pref. above, Thryallis draws attention to τὸ μήτε ὑπέρογκον μήτ' ἄσαρκον of her hips. Jacobs[1] x 155.

1 περιλάμβανε: this verb for *embrace* is very rare in the epigrammatists; Automedon 5.129.7 = *PG* 1515 γλωττίζει, κνίζει, περιλαμβάνει, Nicarchus 5.38.3 ἡ μὲν γάρ με νέα περιλήψεται; *cf.* Lucian *dial. meretr.* 4.2 περιλαμβάνουσαν, ἐπιστρέφουσαν, φιλοῦσαν, 5.4 ὥσπερ ἄνδρα περιελάμβανον. **ἰσχνήν:** *cf.* Argentarius 5.102.1 = *PG* 1319 τὴν ἰσχνὴν Διόκλειαν, ἀσαρκοτέρην 'Αφροδίτην.

2 μεσότητα: a rare word in poetry; Bassus 10.102.3 = *PG* 1633 αἱ μεσότητες ἄρισται, Palladas 10.51.5 ἡ μεσότης γὰρ ἄριστον.

The commonest preference at all times (at least in the poets) was not for the mean between fat and thin but for the slender as opposed to the middle-weight, and the favourite adjective is ῥαδινή (*e.g.* Theocr. 10.24, Meleager 5.173.3 = *PG* 4144, Agathias 5.218.6, 5.220.6, 5.282.1, 5.292.12; of a bridegroom, Sappho *fr.* 115.2).

3 χύσις: LSJ make a special category for this example, *quantity, abundance*; the use is a slight extension of their II 2, *heap*, as in Hom. *Od.* 5.483, of leaves, Nic. *Ther.* 297, of a heap of straw.

XIV

A woman, caught with a lover, is thrashed and evicted. See XVI Pref.

The only other epigrams in the Anthology on anything like this theme are Agathias 5.218, on Polemon and his wife Rhodanthe (but Polemon does not turn her out of the house) and 5.220. A better parallel is Philostr. *epist. amat.* 61 (64) *init.* τίς σε, ὦ καλή, περιέκειρεν; ὡς ἀνόητος καὶ βάρβαρος ὁ μὴ φεισάμενος τῶν 'Αφροδίτης δώρων...φεῦ ἀναιδοῦς παλάμης· ὄντως πάντα τὰ ἐκ πολεμίων πέπονθας. *Cf.* Lucian *dial. meretr.* 8. Jacobs[1] x 172–3, [2]xiii 67, [3]v 58; Hecker 1843, 35–6.

1 ἔδειρεν: as in XVI 6, *thrash*, a colloquial and Comic use.

2 λιθίνην: "λίθος, πέτρος, *saxum, lapis*, etc. are proverbial for insensitivity to emotion", as Gow says on Theocr. 3.18; *cf.* Theocr. 23.20 λάινε παῖ καὶ ἔρωτος ἀνάξιε, Alciphron 4.16 (2.1) 7 οὐχ οὕτως εἰμὶ λιθίνη, Lucian *dial. meretr.* 12.2 λίθος, οὐκ ἄνθρωπός ἐστι, 'Aeschines' *epist.* 10 λίθινος ὑπ' ἀπιστίας ἐγεγόνειν, LXX Ez. 11.19 λιθίνην καρδίαν; Headlam on Herodas 6.4.

οὐκ ἔβλεπεν: *had no eyes, was blind to your beauty; cf.* Strato 12.189.2 ὄμματα καὐτὸς ἔχει, *he too has eyes*, Ach. Tat. 6.21.3 οὐδεὶς αὐτῶν εἶχεν ὀφθαλμούς, 5.26.6 δοκῶ, Θέρσανδρος τυφλὸς ἦν; Ovid *am.* 3.3.42 *di quoque habent oculos.*

3 μοιχόν: as in xvi 1 and 2; both noun and verb are avoided by the earlier epigrammatists; in *HE* only anon. 9.520.2 = 3925, in *PG* only Argentarius 7.403.8 = 1484.

ἀκαίρως: here and in xxv 1 Rufinus breaks the rule, generally observed from the beginning of the Alexandrian era, that, if the fourth foot of the hexameter is spondaic, no word except a prospective monosyllable may end with that foot (Naeke's law; Maas *metr.* §92). Exceptions are rare: Callimachus *Del.* 226 (where Maas emends), Nic. *Ther.* 457; in *HE*, only Aratus 12.129.3 = 762, Leonidas 6.288.1 = 2213, Nicarchus 7.159.3 = 2749; in *PG*, only Archias 7.214.7 = *PG* 3730; in the *Cycle*, only Barbucallus *Plan.* 38.3; in Lucillius and Nicarchus, only 11.309.5; Strato has six examples, Palladas four.

Adverbial ἀκαίρια would have suited the metre and may be the original reading; the word is very rare, but *cf.* Peek 1571.11 (IV A.D.) μέγ' ἀκαίριος ἥκεις.

4 γινόμενον: *it* (*sc.* τὸ μοιχεύειν) *is the usual thing. Cf.* Demosth. 24.83 τὸ γιγνόμενον (*sc.* τίμημα), *the customary* (fine), 38.25 οὐ δικαίαν οὐδὲ γιγνομένην (*usual*) χάριν, Xen. *Cyr.* 5.4.51 ἐν ταῖς γιγνομέναις (*customary*) ἡμέραις. I know no exact parallel to the use of the participle here (Professor Sandbach and Dr Dawe both doubt it), but there is no other possible interpretation of the text, and no emendation is worth consideration (κλινόμενον Hecker).

5 ἀπὸ νῦν: I know no exact parallel to the phrase, but analogies are quoted by LSJ *s.v.* 1 1, *e.g.* ἀπὸ τοῦ νῦν, μέχρι (τοῦ) νῦν.

ὅταν ἐστίν: see the Introduction, p. 43.

6 σφήνου: not *close the vestibule*, as LSJ, but *wedge the front-door*. It is not enough to close or even to lock the door; it is advisable to put a wedge in. σφηνόω could not be used of shutting a door, and is not in fact used of bolting or locking one.

XV

Woman should be neither too wanton nor too modest.

A commonplace theme, illustrated in the note on Philodemus 12. 173.5–6 = *PG* 3258–9.

Jacobs[1] x 178.

1 ἀφελῆ: see the Introduction, p. 47.

XVI

A woman caught with a lover and expelled.

A woman visited by a *moechus* is not necessarily a wife (Professor Sandbach compares Men. *Pk.* 200, 408 K.). The identity of the speakers in xiv and xvi is not clear, but xvi 5, 'We will find you another lover', suggests a complaisant mother or a procuress and supports the opinion that the subject of the epigram is not a wife but a wayward girl; the address τέκνον, once in xiv and twice in xvi, is suitable.

Jacobs¹ x 173–4, ³v 59.

2 ἀπὸ Πυθαγόρου: for the phrase, *cf.* LSJ *s.v.* ἀπό iii 1 *c.* Cf. Diog. Laert. 8.9 καὶ περὶ ἀφροδισίων δέ φησιν (ὁ Πυθαγόρας) οὕτως· "ἀφροδίσια χειμῶνος ποιέεσθαι, μὴ θέρεος· φθινοπώρου δὲ καὶ ἦρος κουφότερα, βαρέα δὲ πᾶσαν ὥραν καὶ ἐς ὑγιείην οὐκ ἀγαθά." ἀλλὰ καί ποτ' ἐρωτηθέντα πότε δεῖ πλησιάζειν εἰπεῖν "ὅταν βούληι γενέσθαι σεαυτοῦ ἀσθενέστερος"; 8.19 οὐδέποτ' ἐγνώσθη οὔτε διαχωρῶν οὔτε ἀφροδισιάζων οὔτε μεθυσθείς; Martial 9.47.3–4.

3 καταδρύψεις: κατατρίψεις, the reading of P, *rub away*, seems unnatural in the context, and the verb is not so used elsewhere. Planudes would not have found fault with it, and I suppose that his reading comes to him from a source independent of P. καταδρύπτω is the right word: Hes. *scut.* 243 κατὰ δ' ἐδρύπτοντο παρειάς, E. *Hec.* 655 δρύπτεται παρειάν, *El.* 150 δρύπτε κάρα, Xen. *Cyr.* 3.1.13 γυναῖκες ἀναβοήσασαι ἐδρύπτοντο, Ap. Rhod. 3.672 δρύψεν δ' ἑκάτερθε παρειάς, Perses 7.487.3 = *HE* 2881 καταδρύψασα παρειάς, Ach. Tat. 1.12.5 τὸ πρόσωπον... περιδρύπτεται.

4 παραριγώσεις: the compound here only. For the prosody, παράριγ-, *cf.* Antiphilus 9.14.3 = *PG* 967, Automedon 5.129.7 = *PG* 1515, Lucillius 11.206.5, Palladas 9.174.6 and 9.441.2, Agathias 9.769.4.

5 ἔκμαξαι: a rare compound; of wiping away blood, S. *El.* 446, E. *H.F.* 1400.

χεὐρήσομεν: asyndeton between the imperatives and the future tense would have been normal; perhaps καὶ is not connective but emphatic, stressing εὑρήσομεν ἄλλον.

6 Jacobs' correction seems indispensable, but μὴ καὶ...καὶ..., equivalent to μήτε...μήτε..., is, as Dr Dawe observes, very strange.

XVII

On two dockside harlots.

An imitation of Asclepiades (or Hedylus) 5.161 = *HE* xl. The words τὰ λῃστρικὰ τῆς Ἀφροδίτης φεύγετε are taken unchanged from the model, a most unusual phenomenon,¹ particularly surprising in so independent a phrase-maker as Rufinus.

The description of harlots in terms of sea-faring is commonplace; *cf.* Alcaeus Mitylen. *fr.* 306 (14), Meleager 5.204 = *HE* lx, Antiphilus 9.415 = *PG* xliii, Philip 9.416 = *PG* lii.

¹ *Cf.* Gaetulicus 7.244.4, where Θυρέα δ' ἦσαν ἄεθλα δορός is taken *verbatim* from Chaeremon 7.721.2 = *HE* 1368.

This epigram and its model are hard to find in Jacobs[1]: Asclepiades *l.c.* appears as 'Simonides lviii', and Rufinus xvii as 'Nicarchus iii' (though Jacobs admits that the epigram should be restored to Rufinus).

1 The women take their names from boats called κέρκουρος and λέμβος; these are described in detail by Torr *Ancient Ships* (Cambridge 1894) 110–11 and 115–16.

2 *Cf.* Thuc. 7.3.5 τριήρης...ἐφορμοῦσα τῶι λιμένι.

See 1 Pref.; 'the' harbour of the Samians will be the famous one of which Herodotus writes, 3.60.3.

3 πανδημί: the suffix -ί conforms to the rule, discussed at great length by Blomfield in his Glossary on [A.] *P.V.* 216 (*cf.* Jebb on S. *O.C.* 1251), that nouns in -η and -α make adverbs in -εί, nouns in -ος make adverbs in -ί. There are many exceptions to the rule, *e.g.* A. *S.c.T.* 296 and *Eum.* 1038 πανδημεί.

4 συμμίξας: of joining battle, as in Thuc. 1.49.1 ξυμμείξαντες, 8.104.4 ξυμμεῖξαι.

καί: giving emphasis to the phrase καταδὺς πίεται, as Dübner says; not *he who engages, and is sunk, is swallowed up*, as Paton.

πίεται: a rare metaphor, whether of the sea *swallowing* a ship (Theognis 680 μή πως ναῦν κατὰ κῦμα πίηι), or of the harlot *swallowing* somebody's money (Ar. *Ran.* 1466 πλήν γ' ὁ δικαστὴς αὐτὰ καταπίνει μόνος; *cf. Vesp.* 1147); both ideas together, as here, Anaxil. *fr.* 22.18–19 ἡ δὲ Φρύνη... | τόν τε ναύκληρον λαβοῦσα καταπέπωκ' αὐτῶι σκάφει.

Parallels to the prosody of πῑεται are assembled in the note on Apollonides 11.25.5 = *PG* 1283 πῑόμεσθα.

XVIII

Rufinus too sleepy to make love.

This is an original variation on a common theme, in which the conventional cause is not sleepiness but impotence (Automedon 11.29 = *PG* ii, Philodemus 11.30 = *PG* xxvii, Scythinus 12.232, Strato 12.11 and 216, Ovid *am.* 3.7.65, Tibullus 1.5.39, Martial 12.86).

Jacobs[1] x 155–6.

1 ἡρασάμην: *vowed*, despite the scansion; see the Introduction, p. 41.

ἐν νυκτί: perhaps better taken with λαβών than with πληρῶσαι.

Θάλεια: a rare name; Agathias 7.568.2.

2 ἐρωμανίηι: see the Introduction, p. 47.

4 ὑπναλέωι: not a common word; Pindar *Pae.* 8.34 (a probable supplement),

Nic. *Ther.* 162, *Al.* 85. Not in *HE*, in *PG* only Bianor 9.227.6 = 1688, in the *Cycle* Macedonius 5.243.7.

5 θυμέ: θυμός here presumably stands for *membrum virile* as in Hipponax *fr.* 10 (Masson) ἐν δὲ τῶι θυμῶι | ...ἑπτάκις ῥαπισθείη and in Palladas 11.317.1 ὄνον μακρόθυμον. See Degani *Studi Classici in onore di Qu. Cataudella* 1 (1972) 97.

6 ζητήσεις: *desiderabis, seek but not find*, as in Plut. *Galb.* 8 φοβεῖται μὴ τάχα Νέρωνα ζητήσωσι, Hdt. 1.94.4 μὴ ζητέοιεν σῖτα, Peek 1474.3 (I A.D.) ζητούμενος οἷς ἀπέλειπες. The implication is 'later on you will be sorry that you missed such an opportunity – you will look for it in vain'.

ὑπερευτυχίην: here only, but Vettius Valens has ὑπερευτυχής; *cf.* ὑπερευγενής and ὑπερευδαιμονεῖν (Aristotle), ὑπερευκαιρέουσα (Hippocrates); Peek 226.2 (II A.D.) has πανευτυχίην.

XIX

A woman ageing but still beautiful.

This epigram and XXIII are variations on a common theme; *cf.* Asclepiades 7.217 = *HE* xli, Philodemus 5.13 = *PG* ii, Paulus 5.258, Agathias 5.282.

Jacobs[1] x 178–9.

1 ὄμματα...χρύσεια: χρύσεος and χρύσ(ε)ο- regularly signify either *golden* (or at least *valuable as gold*) or *gold-coloured*. The use here, in IX 1, and in XXI 1, simply *bright, shining*, is not common; Rhianus 12.93.5 = *HE* 3212 χρύσεον ῥέθος, Peek 1938.9 (II A.D.) στόμα...τὸ χρύσεον.

ὑαλόεσσα: see XII 7 n.; the word here only.

3 λυγδινέη: see X 2 n.

μαρμαίροντα: *gleaming*; Rufinus has varied the phrasing of Homer, *Il.* 3.397 στήθεά θ' ἱμερόεντα καὶ ὄμματα μαρμαίροντα. Elsewhere of the face, Alciphron 3.31 (67).1 αἱ παρειαὶ μαρμαίρουσιν, Agathias 5.282.3 μαρμαίρουσι παρηίδες.

4 ἀργυρέης...Θέτιδος: Hom. *Il.* 1.538 ἀργυρόπεζα Θέτις, taken by Rufinus to mean *with silvery feet*; *cf.* XXI 1 παρθένος ἀργυρόπεζος.

5 ἄκανθαι: thistledown may be called hair (Theocr. 6.15–16 ὡς ἀπ' ἀκάνθας | ταὶ καπυραὶ χαῖται, *like the dry hair of the thistle*), but white hair is not elsewhere called thistledown; *notanda metaphora de canis*, said Jacobs, who could find no parallel. It is not white hair that is meant by ἄκανθαι in anon. *A.P.* 12.40.3 = *HE* 3700, nor probably in the obscure phrase in [S.] *fr.* 1121 Pearson τὰς ἀκάνθας ἐπεγείροντα.

6 καλάμης: *cf.* Asclepiades 12.36.3–4 = *HE* 1028–9 καί τίς ἂν εἴποι | κρείσσονας αὐχμηρὰς ἀσταχύων καλάμας;, Philip 11.36.6 = PG 3032 τὴν καλάμην δωρῆι, δοὺς ἑτέροις τὸ θέρος, Flaccus 12.25.6 = PG 3850 σταχύων ἀντιδιδοὺς καλάμην, Strato 12.215.2 καὶ καλάμη γὰρ ἔσηι, Aristot. *rhet.* 1410b14 ἡ δὲ μεταφορὰ ποιεῖ τοῦτο μάλιστα· ὅταν γὰρ εἴπηι τὸ γῆρας καλάμην κτλ. (= Hom. *Od.* 14.213–14 καλάμην γέ σ' ὀίομαι εἰσορόωντα | γιγνώσκειν).

οὐδὲν ἐπιστρέφομαι: a ready-made pentameter-end; Theognis 440, Asclepiades 12.153.2 = HE 899, Antiphilus 9.413.5–6 = PG 831–2, Automedon 11.319.6 = PG 1540.

XX

Love is harder to endure than poverty.
This epigram is translated by Claudian *carm. min.* xv; see the Introduction, p. 21.

XXI

A girl bathing.
The theme has no parallel in the Anthology. In Asclepiades (or Posidippus) 5.209 = HE xxxvi a man is enamoured of a girl whom he sees swimming, but there is no other resemblance between the epigrams. Jacobs[1] x 156–7.

1–2 ἀργυρόπεζος: for ἀργυρόπεζα, here only; compounds in -πεζος are very rare. *Cf.* xix 4.

χρωτὶ γαλακτοπαγεῖ: *arcte cum* χρύσεα *iungenda*, said Jacobs, and indeed there is no other construction for the dative. χρύσεα means in effect *bright* (see xix 1 n.), and the phrase here is a variation of μαζοὶ λευκότητι λαμπροί; *cf.* Hdt. 4.64.3 (δέρμα) λευκότατον λαμπρότητι.

γαλακτοπαγεῖ = *milk-white*; -παγεῖ is without force, as in Strato 12.204.4 ἄρνα γαλακτοπαγῆ, *milk-white lamb*. In Peek 1884.2 (A.D. 41), γλακτοπαγεῖ μαστῶι, the meaning is *compact with milk*.

μῆλα: 'apples', of the breasts; *cf.* Ar. *Lys.* 155, *Eccl.* 903, Theocr. 27.50, Paulus 5.258.3–4, and Leonidas 6.211.3 = HE 1961 μηλοῦχον.

3–4 ἀλλήλαις: the dative can only be of competition (Kühner–Gerth I 432), εἱλίσσοντο representing ἑλισσόμεναι ἡμιλλῶντο, as ἐδίσκεον ἀλλήλοισι in Hom. *Od.* 8.188 stands for δισκοῦντες ἡμιλλῶντο ἀλλήλοις. The movement of one buttock is opposed to that of the other; they turn against each other. Lamentable conjectures for ἀλλήλαις are assembled by Sternbach (ἀλλήλως, ἀλλάγδην, and worse).

The phrasing recalls Ap. Rhod. 3.138 ἀψῖδες περιηγέες εἱλίσσονται.

ὑγροτέρωι χρωτί: another loose dative, presumably with σαλευόμεναι, *vibrating with flesh more liquid than water*. The phrase recalls Philip 9.709.6 = PG 3057 χαλκὸν...ὕδατος ὑγρότερον; it is presumably mere coincidence that the epigrams which have this phrase in common are both concerned with the river Eurotas.

5–6 ὑπεροιδαίνοντα here only; Lucian has ὑπεροιδάω.

κατέσκεπε: cf. Lucian *merc. cond.* 42 τῆι ἑτέραι...τὴν αἰδῶ σκέπω. The verb is quite common in prose of the early centuries A.D. and appears occasionally in the poets (Antiphilus 6.250.7 = *PG* 789, Agathias 5.294.4).

οὐχ ὅλον Εὐρώταν: the meaning is obvious but the expression is unintelligible. What a girl tries to hide in such circumstances is the *pubes* (Ovid *A.A.* 2.613 *ipsa Venus pubem, quotiens velamina ponit,* | *protegitur laeva semireducta manu*) but neither *pubes* nor *pudenda* are elsewhere called Εὐρώτας (the Suda and Eustathius know the use only from this passage), nor is there any apparent reason why they should be. *A nimia Veneris usu* εὐρυτιώσης, said Jacobs, approved by Waltz, forgetting that the girl is παρθένος; moreover a connection with εὐρυτιάω or εὐρὺς would have to be related to the *pudenda*, not the *pubes*.

Mention of the river should be connected somehow with the fact that the girl is bathing, but the point remains wholly obscure.

XXII

A joke for Philippa.

The point of the epigram was defined correctly by Hecker: *gloriatur se, cum iam duodecies cum Philippa Veneri operatus esset, rursus postero die eundem numerum expleturum, sed quum haec postero die venisset, se vel eadem nocte illud facere potuisse dixit; i.e.* after prodigious feats today he promises the same tomorrow; when she comes the next day, he says that he regrets the waste of time in the interval.

Jacobs[1] x 157–8, [2]xiii 65; Hecker 1843, 42–3.

1 κυανοβλεφάρωι: the compound here only; κυάνοφρυς Theocritus.

παίζων κόνδακα: the word κόνδαξ appears elsewhere only in the Code of Justinian (iii 4.3.1, *Corp. Jur. Civ.* ii ed. P. Krueger) and the *Nomocanon* (13.28.1, quoted by Krueger *l.c.*). The code has it under the heading *de aleae lusu et aleatoribus* among five exceptions to a general prohibition of games of chance; after the general prohibition the section continues *deinde vero ordinent quinque ludos, ton monobolon, ton condomonobolon, ke kondacca ke repon ke perichyten* (a transliteration of τὸν μονόβολον, τὸν κονδομονόβολον, καὶ κόνδακα καὶ ῥέπον καὶ περιχυτήν). The *Nomocanon* runs μόνον δὲ παίζειν ἔξεστι μονόβολον καὶ κονδομονόβολον (μονίβ- and κονδομονίβ- codd.) καὶ κουιντανὸν καὶ κόνδακα χωρὶς τῆς πόρπης (ἄρπης some codd.) καὶ περιχυτὴν καὶ ἱππικὴν ἄνευ τέχνης καὶ ἐπινοίας; this account differs in adding ἱππικὴν and omitting ῥέπον, and in naming six games instead of five; editors therefore write κουιντανὸν κόνδακα instead of κουιντανὸν καὶ κόνδακα.

The nature of the game is unknown. The heading *alea* in the Code and the phrase δώδεκά σοι βέβληκα in Rufinus suggest at first sight a dicing-game; but *alea* in the jurists covers games of chance in general, and the phrase χωρὶς πόρπης would seem to rule out dicing. Moreover the great throw in dicing was three sixes, not two.

Balsamon comments on the *Nomocanon*, Κυϊντανὸς χωρὶς τῆς πόρπης, ὁ ἀκοντισμὸς χωρὶς περόνης ἤγουν σιδήρου, ἀπὸ Κυΐντου τινὸς οὕτω κληθείς, and this is the explanation accepted by LSJ, *a gambling game played with an unpointed dart*; but πόρπη is a *fibula*, a clasp, not a point, and I have no confidence in the explanation of *quintanus*.

If κόνδαξ was some kind of spear or dart, it would suit the context much better than dicing. It seems very rash to identify it with the pole-throwing game described by Pollux 9.120 under the quite different name κυνδαλισμός (Jacobs, followed by Dübner; doubted by Kroll, *RE* 16.129).

Φιλίππηι: dative of competition (E. *Andr.* 127 δεσπόταις ἁμιλλᾶι; xxi 3 n. above), *playing against Philippa.*

2 *durissimum certe est in his mente supplere* λέγων, said Dübner, and Stadtmüller and Waltz accept the conjectures ἡδὺ γελῶν (Reiske) and ἐβόων (Bernard). Hecker judged differently: *dura quidem est omissio verbi* ἔλεγον, *sed quum bis in eodem carmine occurrat, sine dubio ab ipso profecta Rufino.* The decision is not easy. The omission of the verb of *saying* is awkward, and so is a construction which makes it necessary in 2 to understand αὐτὴν from Φιλίππηι in 1 (hence Herwerden changed the datives in 1 to accusatives). The text has, however, one considerable advantage over the conjecture: it is likelier that the *laughter from the heart* so fully described is that of the girl than of the man; it is he who makes the joke, her laughter which is the expected consequence. If it were his own laugh, it would probably have been less fulsomely described (thus, briefly, γελάσας in 5, when he laughs at his own joke). Moreover the conjecture ἐβόων for ἐπόουν is rather ingenious than probable.

ἐξ αὐτῆς κραδίης: cf. Julian *Athen.* 284D ἀπ' αὐτῆς...στένων τῆς καρδίας. For the construction γελᾶν (αὐτὴν) ἐπόουν, see LSJ *s.v.* ποιέω II 1 *b.*

4 ἐπισταμένως Hecker, without need.

5 The hiatus in κελευομένη ἦλθεν is of a type extremely rare in the literary epigram; so rare, that it should not be accepted if there is an easy remedy. Ludwich's neat conjecture has the merits of mending the metre, supplying the desired verb *I said* for 3-4, and making it easier to supply the same verb for 6.

6 ἐγρομένην: ἐρχομένην is ruled out by the context; Paton's rendering, 'I wish I had called you at night too *when you were coming*', is correct, and a sufficient proof that the text is corrupt. Jacobs (*Addenda* 13.65) was the first to see that ἐρχομένην is incoherent; Stadtmüller's easy and convincing emendation appears in the text of Waltz, but not in Paton, Beckby, or Stadtmüller himself.

XXIII

A woman ageing but still beautiful; see XIX Pref.
Jacobs[1] x 158–9, [2]xIII 65; Hecker 1843, 34–5.

1 ἔσβεσεν: of the destruction of beauty also in anon. 12.39.1 = *HE* 3782 ἐσβέσθη Νίκανδρος; *cf.* Dionysius 7.78.1–2 = *HE* 1441–2 γῆράς σε... ἔσβεσεν, Antipater of Sidon 7.30.5 = *HE* 280 οὐδ' 'Αίδης σοι ἔρωτας ἀπέσβεσεν.

2 λείψανα...ἡλικίης: *cf.* Palladas 11.54.1–2 γηραλέον με γυναῖκες ἀποσκώπτουσι λέγουσαι | εἰς τὸ κάτοπτρον ὁρᾶν λείψανον ἡλικίης.

3–4 ἱλαρῶν μήλων: *merry breasts* is not a credible expression, and μῆλα must be *cheeks*, as in Zonas 9.556.4 = *PG* 3489 φοινιχθεὶς μᾶλα παρηΐδια, where the adjective helps, and in Lucian, *imag.* 6, where τὰ μῆλα, *cheeks*, are unqualified.

ἱλαρός as an epithet for the cheeks is easy to understand but hard to exemplify. The adjective is rare in *HE* (only with φωνή, Χάριτες, λάτρις, βλέπειν) and *PG* (only ἱλαροῖς ἐλέγοισιν); Strato has a *cheerful kiss*, 12.16.3 ἱλαροῦ μετάδος τι φιλήματος. Headlam on Herodas 1.40 illustrates the adjective in amatory contexts, but there is no example of its application to a part of the body; closest Lucian *amor.* 3 ἱλαραὶ μὲν τῶν ὀμμάτων αἱ βολαί.

ἢ ῥόδον: οὐ ῥόδον Boissonade, an elegant conjecture, but there is no need for change; *nor has the beauty* (κάλλος for καλόν Jacobs, an unnecessary change) *or the rose of your merry cheeks fled away.* ἢ ῥόδου (Hecker) is no improvement, ἠρινὸν (Jacobs) is mere re-writing.

5 κατέφλεξε: *cf.* Alcaeus 5.10.3 = *HE* 40 τί πλέον, εἰ θεὸς ἄνδρα καταφλέγει;, Polystratus 12.91.7 = *HE* 3046 καίεσθε τρύχεσθε καταφλέχθητε, Meleager 12.127.3 = *HE* 4422 διπλαῖ δ' ἀκτῖνές με κατέφλεγον, anon. *A.P.* 5.2.1 τὴν καταφλεξίπολιν Σθενελαΐδα.

θεοείκελον: not in *HE* or *PG*.

κάλλος: ἄνθος in the *apographa* is a conjecture, and inferior to the suggestion of Jacobs (*Addenda* 13.65) τὸ πρίν, θεοείκελε, κάλλος.

Here as occasionally elsewhere (sometimes with gross errors of prosody) the Corrector has made up a couple of alternatives to fill the gap.

XXIV

The poet implores Prodica to save him from dying of love for her. There is no close parallel to the theme.
Jacobs[1] x 176, [3]v 60; Hecker 1843, 43–4.

1 μονάσασαν: see the Introduction, p. 47.

2 ἀμβροσίων: the adjective implies divinity. "ἀμβρόσιος of the human body

94

COMMENTARY: XXIV–XXV

not, I think, before Ap. Rhod. (3.834, 868)", Barrett on E. *Hipp.* 135–8, p. 187; nor is it commonly so used later. In *HE*, only Hedylus 6.292.3–4 = 1827–8 ἦν γὰρ Ἐρώτων | καὶ Χαρίτων ἡ παῖς ἀμβρόσιόν τι θάλος, in *PG* only Philodemus 5.13.5–6 = 3170–1 χρὼς...ἔτ' ἀμβροσίην, ἔτι πειθώ | πᾶσαν, ἔτι στάζει μυριάδας Χαρίτων. Rufinus addresses Prodica as a goddess, praying for rescue as one prays to the Olympians; *cf.* anon. *A.P.* 5.11.1–2, addressed to Aphrodite, κάμὲ... σῶσον ἀπολλύμενον.

4 Variation of conventional phrasing, Meleager 5.195.7 = *HE* 4122 βαιὸν ἔχω τό γε λειφθὲν...πνεῦμα, Asclepiades 12.166.1 = *HE* 888 τοῦθ' ὅ τί μοι λοιπὸν ψυχῆς; *cf.* Meleager 12.72.2 = *HE* 4491, 12.159.2 = *HE* 4563.

5 *Cf.* Nonnus *D.* 8.205 δάκρυον...ἀποψήσασα, Paulus *ecphr.* 171 δάκρυ' ἀποψήσαντες.

6 ὑπεξέλαβεν: no editor accepts Hecker's conjecture (he himself preferred an inferior alternative, χερσὶ πέριξ ἔλαβεν), but I have no doubt that it is correct. The fact that she wept and then wiped away her tears indicates that she was moved by his prayer and relented. The tone of the whole is consistent only with relenting, not with repelling; ὑπεξέβαλεν would be παρὰ προσδο-κίαν, quite out of place in this epigram and inconsistent with the tone of τρυφεραῖς χερσίν. It may be thought too that the action described by ὑπεξέβαλεν (*warf mich hinaus*, Beckby; *me mit à la porte*, Waltz) is too rough for the context; nor is the verb itself convincing: ὑπεκβάλλω occurs only in Ap. Rhod. 1.596, ὑπὲκ ποταμοῖο βαλεῖν Ἀμύροιο ῥέεθρα, where the verb seems to mean something like *put on one side*, *i.e.* pass away from. Here ὑπεξ-implies *from my humble posture* (kneeling, 2).

XXV

Athena and Hera, seeing the beauty of Maeonis, are glad that she will not be their rival in a second judgement of Paris.

The motif has no precedent in the Anthology; it is repeated in Agathias 5.222.5–6 εἰ δὲ καὶ ἀγλαΐης κρίσις ἵστατο, μᾶλλον ἂν αὐτῇ | Κύπρις ἐνικήθη κἀνεδίκαζε Πάρις. *Cf.* Philostratus *epist. amat.* 62 (66) ὅτε δὲ ἔκρινε τὰς θεὰς ὁ Ἀλέξανδρος, οὔπω παρῆν ἡ ἐκ Λακεδαίμονος· εἰ δ' οὖν, μόνην ἂν καλὴν ἀπεφήνατο κτλ.

Jacobs[1] x 172.

1 καὶ Ἥρη: for the metrical anomaly (breach of Naeke's law) see XIV 3 n.

χρυσοπέδιλος: conventional epithet for Hera; Hom. *Od.* 11.604, Hes. *Theog.* 454.

2 Μαιονίδα: as a proper-name here only; comparable with *e.g.* Λύδη, Φρυγία used as proper-names.

4 ἡττᾶσθαι: the word is avoided by the Alexandrians and their followers. It

95

does not occur in Callimachus or Theocritus; in *HE*, only Mnasalces 6.264.6 = 2626 ἀήσσατος, in *PG* only Crinagoras 7.741.8 = 1890 ἀήττητον, where the form with ττ is offered as in Rufinus, in Nicarchus 11.110.8 ἥττημαι, and in Palladas 9.441.4 ἡττηθείς.

καλλοσύνης: καλλοσύνη, for κάλλος, is surprisingly rare in literature; καλλοσύνη ἐπέων, title of a book by Democritus, 2.91.25 D.–K.; E. *Hel.* 383, *Or.* 1387; in *HE*, only Meleager 5.195.2 = 4211; in *PG*, only Antipater of Thessalonica *Plan.* 75.5 = 335 (Honestus 5.20.4 = 2403 is corrupt); in the *Cycle* only Macedonius 11.370.2 νοθοκαλλοσύνη. It may have been much commoner than this record suggests: Peek 767.4 and 1553.4, both I B.C., 643.8, I A.D., 1990.8, II–III A.D.

XXVI

The beloved girl has all the virtues of the goddesses, and counts as a fourth Grace.

There are numerous variations on this theme: Rufinus xxxv, Callimachus 5.146 = *HE* xv, Meleager 5.140, 5.149, 5.195 = *HE* xxx, xxxii, xxxix, anon. *A.P.* 5.95 and 9.515, Strato 12.181, Macedonius 5.231, Paulus 5.260.7–8, Leontius *Plan.* 288, Peek 1925.3–5 (I A.D.?) μορφᾶς ἅι πρωτεῖον ἔχειν δωρήσατο Κύπρις, | ἔργα δ' Ἀθαναία τερπνὰ σαοφροσύνας, | Μοῦσα δὲ καὶ σοφίαν καὶ πακτίδα, 2008.11–12 (early I A.D.) *cui formam Paphie, Charites tribuere decorem,* | *quam Pallas cunctis artibus eruduit*; Weinreich, *Studien zu Martial* (Stuttgart 1928) 19.

Jacobs[1] x 164–5.

1 σῶμα καὶ ἀκμήν: = σώματος ἀκμήν (conjectured by Desrousseaux).

3 χεῖρας Ἀθήνης: χεῖρας here surely connotes the *skill* of her hands; *cf.* Prop. 3.20.7 *est tibi forma potens, sunt castae Palladis artes.* In xxv 1, however, the same phrase certainly connotes the *beauty* of her hands; *cf.* Rhianus *fr.* 1.14 εὔπηχυν Ἀθήνην.

XXVII

The poet sees Rhodocleia bathing and at first mistakes her for Aphrodite.

The nearest parallel to the theme is Asclepiades 5.209 = *HE* xxxvi, but all they have in common is seeing a girl bathing.

Jacobs[1] x 160–1, [3]v 61.

2 καταυχενίους: the compound here only.

3 ἰλήκοις, δέσποινα: *cf.* Crinagoras 6.253.7 = *PG* 2028 αὐταί θ' ἰλήκοιτε, Philip 6.251.7 = *PG* 2678 ἀνθ' ὧν ἰλήκοις; the motif is particularly common in the *Cycle*, Agathias 6.74.5 ἰλήκοις, Διόνυσε, 9.154.1 ἰλήκοις, Πολιοῦχε, 5.299.10 and *Plan.* 36.2 ἰλήκοις, Paulus 5.301.5 ἵλαθι, κούρη; *cf.* Alciphron *init.* 3.32 (68) θεοὶ μάκαρες, ἰλήκοιτε.

4 τύπον: *cf.* Diodorus 9.405.3 = *PG* 2144 φυῆς ἐρατὸν τύπον.

6 ἐκδέδυκας: for the prosody, see the Introduction, p. 40. The meaning can only be what the editors say, *you have stripped the goddess (of her beauty)*, but the verb is not well suited to a context which immediately suggests its natural meaning, *stripped of her clothes*.

XXVIII

Wreath and woman both flower and fade.

With the theme of this charming epigram compare especially Meleager 5.147 = *HE* xlvi, Argentarius 5.118 = *PG* xi.

Jacobs[1] x 163–4, [3]v 62; Mackail ix 2.

1–2 Planudes' variants are mysterious; there was no need for conjecture, and accident seems unlikely. Probably an ancient (and in our judgement inferior) *varia lectio*.

3–4 A. Harmon in *Class. Phil.* 22 (1927) 219-20 suggested that the initial letters of the first four flowers and the whole of the fifth should be combined to form the word κρανίον, *skull*, a *memento mori* symbolising the theme of the epigram, that life is short. This ingenious but improbable notion is approved by Waltz and Beckby.

ῥοδέη...κάλυξ: *cf.* Theaetetus Scholasticus 10.16.2 ῥοδέων...καλύκων, Marianus 9.669.6 ῥοδέηι...κάλυκι.

νάρκισσος ὑγρός *cf.* Peek 1409.3 (II A.D.?) ὑδατίνη νάρκισσος.

κυαναυγὲς ἴον: *i.e.* ἴον μέλαν; *cf.* Theocritus 10.28 καὶ τὸ ἴον μέλαν ἐστί. Theophr. *HP* 1.13.2 distinguishes τὸ ἴον τὸ μέλαν from τὸ λευκόν (= λευκόϊον).

XXIX

A seduction and its consequences.

There is no other epigram in the Anthology much like this one.

Jacobs[1] x 165, [2]xiii 66.

1 'Ἀμυμώνην: the name elsewhere only of the well-known mythical lady.

'Ἀφροδίτη: 'Ἀφροδίτην, in apposition to 'Ἀμυμώνην, retained by Stadt-müller, Waltz, and Beckby, is stylistically intolerable; it would be possible only if 'Ἀφροδίτην were somehow qualified as in Argentarius 5.102.1 = *PG* 1319 τὴν ἰσχνὴν Διόκλειαν, ἀσαρκοτέρην 'Ἀφροδίτην.

The address to the goddess would be abnormal at the beginning of an epigram unless she is in some way or to some extent involved in the action; *cf. e.g.* Maccius 5.135.1 = *PG* 2494. Here the question in the last line shows that the epigram is wholly addressed to her.

3 προσέπαιζε: see x 3 n.

4 τί πλέον ;: = *quid profuit? Well, that did not help matters*, Paton. See the note on Asclepiades 5.85.1 = *HE* 816.

τὸν πόνον ἠισθάνετο: *she felt the pang*, as Paton, not *elle vit combien je souffrais* as Waltz, or *sie verstand meine Not*, as Beckby. This phrase must be related to τί πλέον;, *what was the good of it?*, i.e. what was the good of her behaving like a shy child? The sense is 'it was no good blushing – the pang of love was not the less felt'.

πόνον: of love, as in Meleager 12.127.7 = *HE* 4426, 12.126.1 = *HE* 4464.

5 ἤνυσα: as in Paulus 5.275.7 ἀνύσσαμεν ἔργον ἔρωτος.

πολλὰ καμών: *by great efforts*, as in Agathias 9.677.1, *Daphnis and Chloe* 1.14.

παρακήκοα: *I have overheard (people saying...)*, as in Hdt. 3.129.3 παρακούσας τις πρότερον ἔτι ἐν Σάρδισι τοῦ... Δημοκήδεος τὴν τέχνην. Elsewhere the verb almost always means either *eavesdrop*, i.e. deliberately overhear (of slaves with their masters, Ar. *Ran.* 750, Lucian *merc. cond.* 37), or *hear imperfectly*, often with the implication *hear but not heed*. *Cf.* Alciphron 1.14 (11).2, of sailors in a sea-fight, τί οὖν... δρῶμεν; φεύγομεν ἢ μένομεν;, Meleager 12.126.6 = *HE* 4469 οὔτε φυγεῖν οὔτε μένειν δύναμαι.

XXX

A woman once beautiful, now old and ugly. See VII Pref.

Jacobs[1] x 166, [2]XIII 66.

1–2 the epithets ἐρατόχροος and εἰαρόμασθος here only, εὔοφρυς elsewhere only Philostr. *Her.* 19.9; the other three are fairly common.

εἰαρόμασθος: presumably as LSJ, *with youthful breasts*; εἰαρο- in compound is very rare and late (εἰαρόεις Manetho 4.275, εἰαροτερπής *Orph. H.* 51.15).

4 οὐδ' ὄναρ: *cf.* [XXXVIII] 4; Headlam on Herodas 1.11. οὐδ' ὄναρ, *not even i a dream*, implying *in no circumstances*, appears first in Plato, *e.g.* Theaetet. 173D σπουδαὶ δὲ ἑταιριῶν ἐπ' ἀρχὰς καὶ σύνοδοι καὶ δεῖπνα... οὐδ' ὄναρ πράττειν προσίσταται αὐτοῖς, of things which they would *never dream* of doing; Demosth. 13.20 γῆν... ὅσην οὐδ' ὄναρ ἤλπισαν, 19.275 ἃ μηδ' ὄναρ ἤλπισαν; Moschus 4.18; Philodemus 5.25.6 = *PG* 3179; anon. *A.P.* 12.99.1 = *HE* 3684; Leon. Alex. *A.P.* 9.344.2; Strato 12.191.1; Cic. *Att.* 1.18.6; Plut. *adv. Colot.* 4, *Philopoem.* 18; similarly οὐδ' or μηδ' ἐν ὀνείρωι Theocr. 20.5, Ap. Rhod. 1.290, Automedon 11.361.5 = *PG* 1565; οὐδ' ἐν ὕπνωι Plut. *prof. virt.* 16, οὐδ' ἐνύπνιον ἰδών Men. *Pk.* 359.

In all the above passages the matter is something which is likelier to occur in a dream than in reality, or of which one would like to dream, or of which it is natural to say *he would never have dreamed of it*. In the present passage the dream is of an improbable sort; οὐδ' ὄναρ has lost its dream-colour and means simply *not at all*. The earliest examples of the use of οὐδ' ὄναρ with its dream-colour quite faded are (a) Herodas 1.11 ἐξ οὗ σε, Γυλλίς, οὐδ' ὄναρ, μὰ τὰς Μοίρας, | πρὸς τὴν θύρην ἐλθοῦσαν εἶδέ τις ταύτην, where the expression is unnatural, for people do not as a rule *dream* of their neighbours paying them visits; οὐδ' ὄναρ here means simply *not at all*, 'nobody saw you come here at all'; (*b*) 'Callimachus' 5.23.4 = *HE* 1330 (see [xxxviii] below) ἐλέου δ' οὐδ' ὄναρ ἠντίασας, where again the expression is unnatural, for cruel persons are not expected to *dream* of being merciful; οὐδ' ὄναρ means simply *not at all*; (*c*) the present passage, where the dream would be of an improbable sort; again the meaning is simply *not at all*.

5 ἀλλοτρίας: she wears a wig, a common object of ridicule, as in Lucillius 11.68.

6 πίθηκος: *cf.* Semonides *fr.* 7.71–3 τὴν δ' ἐκ πιθήκου...|αἴσχιστα μὲν πρόσωπα, Ar. *Eccl.* 1072 πίθηκος ἀνάπλεως ψιμυθίου, Lucillius 11.196.1 τριπιθήκινον, *Daphnis and Chloe* 3.26 βούλεται συγκαθεύδειν πένητι καλῶι ἢ πιθήκωι πλουσίωι, Alciphron 4.6 (1.33).5 ἀρέσκειν γὰρ τοῖς ἐρασταῖς οὐχὶ Μεγάραι καὶ Εὐξίππηι βούλομαι τοῖς πιθήκοις, Palladas 11.353.1 Ἑρμογένους θυγάτηρ μεγάλωι παρέλεκτο πιθήκωι, Plaut. *Mil. glor.* 4.1.42 *pithecium haec est prae illa.*

XXXI

Melissias is reluctant to confess her love.

The epigram has no close precedent in the Anthology; Irenaeus 5.253 has something in common.

On the tiresome repetition of words (βάσις, βάσιες; ἀστατέουσα, ἄστατος) see the Introduction, p. 5 n. 3.

Jacobs[1] x 166–7, [2]xiii 66, [3]v 63.

1 The name Μελισσιάς not elsewhere, but Μέλισσα is common.

2 κέκραγεν: see the Introduction, p. 40; κέκραγ' (Blomfield) may be right.

3–4 It is generally true of Greek poetry that it does not avoid the non-significant repetition of words within a short space, but the repetitions here are extreme examples of this freedom. See the Introduction, p. 5 n. 3.

βάσις: *tread* or *step*, as in Philostr. *epist. amat.* 18 (22) δέξεται τὴν βάσιν ἡ κόνις; *cf.* E. *Hec.* 837 ποδῶν βάσει. βάσεις = *feet* in Antiphilus 9.13[b].2 = *PG* 960.

ἀστατέουσα: the verb is late and very rare; *App. Anthol.* (Cougny) 3.146.4 πόλοιο φορὰν...ἀστατέουσαν, *motum poli instabilem*, Plut. *Crass.* 17 ἀστατούσης χειμῶνι τῆς θαλάσσης, 1 Ep. Cor. 4.11, *Hippiatr.* 3, Vett. Val. 116.30.

ὁρμή: usually of rapid or violent motion, and that is presumably what is meant here; the epigrammatists generally seem to avoid this word (not in *HE* or *PG*, in the *Cycle* only Arabius *Plan.* 144.3.).

ἰοτυπεῖς: *arrow-struck* (*cf.* σῶμα...βελέων δεξάμενον φαρέτρην above). The word elsewhere only in Antiphilus 9.265.1 = *PG* 1231, in the same sense.

βάσιες: *sockets, sedes oculorum*, as in Soranus 1.27 αἱ ἐν ὀφθαλμοῖς βάσεις. For the eyes as the target of Eros' attack, *cf.* Meleager 12.83.4 = *HE* 4345 ἐμοῖς ὄμμασι πῦρ ἔβαλεν, Ach. Tat. 1.4.4 ὀφθαλμὸς γὰρ ὁδὸς ἐρωτικῶι τραύματι (from the arrows of Eros).

5 μητρός: for Aphrodite as the mother of the Πόθοι, see Headlam on Herodas 7.94–5.

εὐστεφάνου Κυθερείης: as in Hom. *Od.* 8.267 ('Αφροδίτης), 288, Hes. *Theog.* 196, *H. Ven.* 175, Theognis 1339; ἐυστ. Κύπριδος anon. 9.325.4 = *HE* 3899.

6 ἀπιθῆ: for ἀπειθῆ, elsewhere only Timo *ap.* Diog. Laert. 2.55 *s.v.l.*, but ἀπιθέω is Homeric, and [A.] *P.V.* 333 has εὐπϊθής.

XXXII

Love should be mutual.

For the theme, *cf.* 'Tibullus' 3.11.13–14 *nec tu sis iniusta, Venus: vel serviat aeque | vinctus uterque tibi, vel mea vincla leva*, and especially *A.P.* 5.68 (Introduction, p. 20 above).

Jacobs[1] x 168, [3]v 64.

1 ἴσχυσας...καῦσαι: ἰσχύω *c. infin.* is rare; Demosth. 17.9 ἰσχύει... πράττειν.

φλόγα...καῦσαι: *burn* means *kindle*, as in Homeric πῦρ κήαντες.

XXXIII

A prayer that old age may soon overtake a proud beauty.
See VII Pref., and *cf.* Strato 12.186.
Jacobs[1] x 168, [2]XIII 66–7, [3]v 65.

1 ὑψοῦται: the verb is very seldom metaphorical; [Plut.] *consol. Apoll.* 103E ῥαιδίως τὰ ὑψηλὰ γίνεται ταπεινὰ καὶ τὰ χθαμαλὰ πάλιν ὑψοῦται.

"χαῖρε": see x 2 n.

2 (and 4) σοβαραῖς: see the Introduction, pp. 44ff.

3 ἐκκρεμάσωμαι: middle for active *metri gratia*. On wreaths hung up by the *exclusus amator* see Headlam on Herodas 2.34–7.

4 πατεῖ...ἴχνεσι: *cf.* Meleager 12.101.4 = *HE* 4543 ποσσὶ πατῶ.

6 κἄν: see the Introduction, pp. 43–4.

XXXIV

The alliance of Bacchus and Eros too strong for Rufinus.

Variation on a common theme; cf. Callimachus 12.118.3–4 = HE 1077–8 ἄκρητος καὶ ἔρως μ' ἠνάγκασαν, Posidippus 12.120 = HE vii, Prop. 1.3.14 hac Amor, hac Liber, durus uterque deus, Ovid A.A. 3.762, Anthol. Lat. π 2.4 unanimi Bacchus Amorque dei, Ach. Tat. 2.3.3 Ἔρως δὲ καὶ Διόνυσος, δύο βίαιοι θεοί, ψυχὴν κατασχόντες ἐκμαίνουσιν κτλ.; other variations in Meleager 12.119 = HE xx, Argentarius 11.26 = PG xxvii.

Jacobs[1] x 169, [2]xiii 67, [3]v 66; Mackail i 7.

1 ὥπλισμαι...λογισμόν: λογισμῶι (Opsopoeus) would be normal, but cf. S. El. 995–6 θράσος...ὁπλίζηι, 1 Ep. Pet. 4.1 τὴν αὐτὴν ἔννοιαν ὁπλίσασθε, Josephus Ant. 6.187 τὸν θεὸν ὥπλισμαι. In general cf. Posidippus 12.120.4 = HE 3081 τὸν παραταξάμενον πρός σε λογισμὸν ἔχω, Meleager 12.117.3 = HE 4094 τί δ' Ἔρωτι λογισμός;, Maccius Plan. 198.3 ληιστὰ λογισμοῦ = PG 2538 (of Eros).

3 θνατός: θνητὸς Stadtmüller; this and φίλαμα in ιιι 1 are the only 'Doric' alphas in Rufinus.

συστήσομαι: of standing to confront an enemy as in Hdt. 6.108.3, A. S.c.T. 509, E. Suppl. 847, Ar. Vesp. 1031.

βοηθόν: poetry used βοηθόος (very rare in the epigrammatists; not in HE, in PG only Archias 10.8.5 = 3762); I have not noticed βοηθός elsewhere in verse except in Peek 1118.1 (IV b.c., of good quality).

4 An allusion to the proverbial μηδ' Ἡρακλῆς πρὸς δύο.

XXXV

Melita has the graces of the goddesses; see xxvi Pref.

Jacobs[1] x 169–70, [3]v 67.

1 ὄμματ'...Ἥρης: Hera was βοῶπις, an epithet generally understood to refer to the beauty of her eyes (Hesych. s.v., μελανόφθαλμος, εὐόφθαλμος; Myth. Lex. 1.2097).

χεῖρας Ἀθήνης: see xxvi 3 n.; here plainly her hands, not her hand-crafts.

2 σφυρὰ...Θέτιδος: see xix 4 n.; the standard epithet for Thetis in the Epic is ἀργυρόπεζα, not εὔσφυρος or τανίσφυρος.

3 τρισόλβιος: cf. Lucian Nigr. 1 μακάριος...καὶ τοῦτο δὴ τὸ ἀπὸ τῆς σκηνῆς ὄνομα τρισόλβιος; in fact τρισόλβιος is very seldom attested in drama (S. fr. 837.1, Ar. Eccl. 1129, Philemon fr. 93.1).

4 ἀθάνατος: so, in similar contexts, Dioscorides 5.55.2 = HE 1484 ἀθάνατος γέγονα, Strato 12.177.6 πῶς ἀποθειωθεὶς πλάзομ᾽ ἐπιχθόνιος;, Prop. 2.14.10 *inmortalis ero, si altera talis erit*, 2.15.39 *fiam inmortalis in illis*.

γαμῶν: the verb does not always imply *marriage* (LSJ *s.v.* 12), and presumably does not here. Planudes᾽ συνὼν is probably the reading of his source: he often bowdlerises, and would certainly not have substituted συνὼν for a verb which *prima facie* means 'marry'.

XXXVI

Love should be mutual; see xxxii Pref.

Jacobs[1] x 174.

1–2 Jacobs quoted Theophyl. Simocat. *epist.* 45 (44 Jacobs), οὐκ ἰσόρροπον ἔχουσιν οἱ Ἔρωτες τὴν πλάστιγγα. ...εἰ μὲν οὖν ἀδικοῦσιν, θεοὶ μὴ κεκλήσθωσαν· εἰ δὲ τὴν προσηγορίαν οὐ ψεύδονται, καὶ τὰς ἀλγηδόνας ἐμοὶ κατὰ τὸ δίκαιον μεριзέτωσαν.

εἶ: monosyllables at pentameter-end are very rare: Meleager 12.63.6 = *HE* 4489 πῦρ, Lucillius 11.95.2 μῦς, Nicarchus 11.241.2 ἦν, Strato 11.225.2 τρεῖς, Barbucallus *Plan.* 219.2 εἶς, five examples in Palladas. Dorieus *ap.* Athen. 10.412F has a monosyllabic enclitic in this position, μοῦνος ἐδαίσατό νιν.

XXXVII

A warning to a heartless beauty that old age will soon overtake her.

See vii Pref.

Jacobs[1] x 175.

1 It is not clear why μέχρι...ἄχρι was written instead of the more rhetorical ἄχρι...ἄχρι (conjectured by Bothe).

παρακλαύσομαι: the epigram is in effect a *paraclausithyron* like [xxxviii]; *cf.* also Asclepiades 5.64, 5.145, 5.164 = *HE* xi–xiii and especially 5.189 = *HE* xlii, Meleager 12.72 = *HE* xcii.

3 σοι: the only example in Rufinus of correption before the feminine caesura; see the Introduction, p. 34.

ἐπισκιρτῶσιν: a very rare compound; with the hair as subject also in Strato 12.10.1 εἰ καί σοι τριχόφοιτος ἐπεσκίρτησεν ἴουλος.

ἔθειραι: the epigrammatists generally avoid this word; in *HE*, only Euphorion 6.279.1 = 1801; in *PG*, only Philodemus 11.41.3 = 3262 and Philip 9.777.4 = 3061; in the *Cycle* only Paulus 5.230.1; also in Strato 12.240.1 and anon. 5.26.1; Peek 746.1 (III–IV A.D.).

4 ὡς Ἑκάβη Πριάμωι: types of the very old; for Hecuba, *cf.* Myrinus 11.67.2 = *PG* 2575 κορωνεκάβη, Lucianus 11.408.6, Martial 3.76.4; for Priam, Juv. 6.325–6, *Priapea* 57.4, Martial 10.67.4.

[XXXVIII]

The best of Rufinus' epigrams are of good quality. The choice between him and some of the most distinguished of his predecessors among the amatory epigrammatists – Asclepiades, for example, or Meleager – might, in a disputed case, be impossible to make with certainty. But one would have expected to be able to distinguish between him and Callimachus.

A.P. 5.23 is ascribed to Callimachus in P. It is headed τοῦ αὐτοῦ, meaning Rufinus, in Planudes, within a long series of epigrams ascribed to Rufinus. The first question to ask is, what may be the authority of Planudes in this place, and the answer has been given in the Introduction, pp. 14ff.: the ascription in Pl is almost certainly the consequence of error of a type very common in Pl; it is prudent to regard the ascription as having no authority whatsoever.

The question remains whether the ascription to Callimachus is acceptable. The reasons given by Pfeiffer, *Callim.* II 99, for rejecting the evidence of P are criticised by F. Zucker in *Philologus* 98 (1954) 94–6 and G. Luck in *CQ* n.s. 6 (1956) 225–30; the cases for and against are, briefly, as follows:

(1) In all Callimachus' amatory epigrams except this one the love is homosexual; Callim. *A.P.* 5.6, which begins with the love of a man for a woman, has its point in its last couplet, νῦν δ' ὁ μὲν ἀρσενικῶι θέρεται πυρί.

We shall agree with Pfeiffer that the theme would be unique in Callimachus; we may agree with Zucker that this observation, though true, is not in itself absolutely decisive.

(2) Certain repetitions of phrase and fact are said to be unlike the style of Callimachus.

On this point Zucker has the advantage. The repetition of οὕτως ὑπνώσαις is a common sort of anaphora which might appear in any good poet; and the repetition of ἐλέου δ' οὐδ' ὄναρ ἠντίασας in σὺ δ' οὐδ' ὄναρ, sc. οἰκτείρεις, is of a similar anaphoric and effective type. There is no need to argue (as Zucker does) that Callimachus has, in other poems, repetitions which modern taste deems inelegant; the only repetition in this epigram which seems dull is that of ὡς τὸν ἐραστὴν κοιμίζεις following ὡς ἐμὲ ποιεῖς κοιμᾶσθαι.

(3) Callimachus avoids *epica correptio* in his epigrams, and ἀδικωτάτη therefore calls for comment.

Though the phenomenon is very rare in the epigrams, it must be admitted that ἀδικωτάτη is not more remarkable than Κλεινίου in *HE* xiv 11 = v 11 Pf. or ἀναπαύεται in *HE* xxxi 1 = xiii 1 Pf., and is less remarkable than the correption of the first short of the dactyl in κεῖται *HE* lxii 2 = lxii 2 Pf. Zucker adds the examples in the Hymns, οὐδέπω, ἁγιωτάτη, ἐκλίθη, in *Del.* 40, 209, 275, and Καϋστρίωι in *Dian.* 257.

(4) Apart from the above points of detail, the *totus dicendi color* of the epigram weighs, for Pfeiffer, heavily in the scale of evidence. He leaves open

the question whether the ascription to Rufinus may be correct, but observes that some of the epigrams's features are reminiscent of Rufinus. And, although it is now clear that the ascription to Rufinus in Pl is the result of mere carelessness, the fact remains that the epigram is in some respects quite like Rufinus:

(a) The theme, *de crine cano*, is particularly common in Rufinus (VII, VIII 5, IX, XIX 5, XXIII, XXX, XXXII 5–6, XXXVII).

(b) The correption of ἀδικωτάτη would be normal in Rufinus.

(c) The apparently careless repetition of word or sense, if there is any, would seem characteristic of Rufinus (see the Introduction, p. 5 n. 3).

So far it appears that both the evidence against Callimachus and that in favour of Rufinus must be judged quite inadequate. I believe that a decisive argument against Callimachus is to be found where it has not hitherto been sought, in the phrase ἐλέου δ' οὐδ' ὄναρ ἠντίασας.

The future ἀντιάσω and the aorist ἠντίασα are occasionally used with the genitive in the sense *meet with*, implying *receive, obtain*: Hom. *Il.* 1.66–7 κνίσης...ἀντιάσας, *Od.* 21.402 ὀνήσιος ἀντιάσειεν, Theognis 1308 Κυπρο-γενοῦς δ' ἔργων ἀντιάσῃς χαλεπῶν, Pind. *Isthm.* 6.15 ἀντιάσαις *sc.* ὧν ἐπεθύμησεν, anon. *A.P.* 9.21.2 ἀδίκου τέρματος ἠντίασα, S. *El.* 869–70 τάφου ἀντιάσας, apparently Callimachus *fr.* 540 χύτλων ἀντιάσαντ-, Peek 871.4 ὁσίων ἀντίασεν κτερέων, 1431.2 πρὶν ζυγίων ἀντιάσαι θαλάμων, 1476.1 δαίμονος ἀντιάσασα κακοῦ, 1508.14–15 γήραος ὡς χαλεποῦ | ἤντησας, 1606.2 ὠδῖνος νύμφη ἀπαντίασεν, 2013.2 ἀλλίστου...ἀντιάσαντ' 'Αΐδεω, 2039.18 στυγεροῦ δαίμονος ἠντίασεν.

The subject of the verb in such examples is always the recipient, never the source, of that which is 'met with'. ἐλέου ἀντιάσας means *encountering compassion*, *i.e.* 'receiving compassion'. It is used of the person pitied; it cannot be used of the person pitying. Boissonade and Bothe seem to have appreciated this fact, for they conjectured ἠντίασα; but σὺ δ' οὐδ' ὄναρ, *sc.* οἰκτίρεις, must refer back to ἐλέου δ' οὐδ' ὄναρ, and the second person ἠντίασας cannot be changed; it may be added that the first person would sit very uncomfortably in the context as a whole.

The consequence must be accepted, that the author of this epigram mistakenly thought that ἐλέου ἀντιάσαι could be used of the person pitying, whereas it can only be used of the person pitied. Few will believe that Callimachus was capable of this misuse. Nor is the ascription to Rufinus made the likelier: his prosody is occasionally outrageous, and his syntax and vocabulary are occasionally closer to the vernacular than is usual in poetry; but no other epigram ascribed to him contains an abuse of language comparable with this.

A few minor arguments are appended:

(1) The words ἔλεος, ἐραστής, ὄναρ, ὑπνόω, ψυχρός are not found in Callimachus.

(2) The phrase οὐδ' ὄναρ here has lost its dream-colour and means

simply *not at all*: it is not to be expected that cruel people will *dream* of being merciful. The earliest example of this watered-down colour is Herodas 1.11; see the note on xxx 3-4 above.

(3) αὐτίκα has been suspected: *ineptissimum, quasi Conopion statim vetula fieret*, said Hecker (1852.203); he conjectured αὖτις, *at some time in the future*, as in *e.g.* Callim. *Jov.* 21, *Lav.* 141, *fr.* 358.2.

It is true that αὐτίκα regularly means *presently*, implying either *now* or *in the near future*; the sense *in the future*, generally, without limitation to the near future, is not recognised by the Lexica, and it is therefore worth noting that this sense is attested in Crinagoras 6.242.5-6 = *PG* 1817-18 καὶ αὐτίκα τῶνδ' ἀπ' Ἰούλων | Εὐκλείδην πολιῆς ἄχρις ἄγοιτε τριχός, where the lapse of time implied by αὐτίκα is from youth to old age, and 9.224.5 = *PG* 1901 ἥξω δ' αὐτίκα που καὶ ἐς ἀστέρας, where the lapse of time is wholly indefinite, *in due course*.

[XXXIX]

Four epigrams by Rufinus precede this one in P; these lines are surely not his work, and it is safe to assume that the heading τοῦ αὐτοῦ is the consequence of mere carelessness. The heading in the Appendix, ἄδηλον, is presumably the true tradition.

INDEXES

1 Rufini verborum index

107

INDEXES

INDEXES

INDEXES

113

INDEXES

II   Index of Subjects